I0283601

Pohick Church

THE HISTORY
OF
TRURO PARISH
IN VIRGINIA

BY

REV. PHILIP SLAUGHTER, D.D.

Edited
With Notes and Addenda
By REV. EDWARD L. GOODWIN
Historiographer of the Diocese of Virginia

CLEARFIELD

Originally published
Philadelphia, Pennsylvania, 1908

Reprinted for
Clearfield Company, Inc. by
Genealogical Publishing Co., Inc.
Baltimore, Maryland
1995, 2003

International Standard Book Number: 0-8063-4601-9

Made in the United States of America

ILLUSTRATIONS

POHICK CHURCH......................	*Frontispiece*	
THE OLD VESTRY BOOK..............	*Facing Page*	34
PAYNES CHURCH, 1768-1862...........	" "	50
ORIGINAL PLAN OF POHICK CHURCH	" "	82
POHICK CHURCH IN THE OLDEN TIME	" "	136

INTRODUCTION

When the English colonists made their first permanent settlement on the shores of Virginia they came to establish themselves as an English people in America. They did not emigrate for purposes of robbery, nor yet to escape conditions which were not to their liking at home, but they brought with them all they could of the old England, including, as a matter of course, the English Church and English law, ecclesiastical and civil. They brought, too, as the event was to prove, the English genius for adapting old forms of government to new conditions of life. Thus in process of time the Parish and the Vestry in Virginia became quite different from the same institutions in the old country, though still based upon the broad sanctions of the ecclesiastical law of England. The Parish was established and its bounds were fixed not by tradition, but by statute, and the Vestry, from an annual meeting of all the ratepayers to choose Churchwardens and discuss parochial affairs, became practically a close corporation of twelve of "The most able and discreet persons" in the Parish. These divided with the County Court the responsibility of local government, having as

INTRODUCTION

their especial charge the maintenance of religion and the oversight of all things pertaining thereto in the domain of charity and morals. These Vestrymen were described by Jefferson as being "Usually the most discreet farmers, so distributed through their Parish that every part of it may be under the eye of some one of them. They are well acquainted with the details and economy of private life, and they find sufficient inducements to execute their charge well in their philanthropy, in the approbation of their neighbors, and the distinction which that gives them."

No Parish in the Colony had a Vestry more distinguished in its personnel, or more fully qualified for their positions, than the Parish of Truro. Of its earlier members indeed little has come down to us but their names inscribed on almost every page of the scant records remaining to tell of the settlement of these upper reaches of the "Northern Neck," and the establishment of religion and civilization in what was then but a wilderness. But later her Vestrymen are found ranking among the first gentlemen of Virginia in position and influence. Eleven of them sat at various times in the House of Burgesses. Two of them, the Fairfaxes, were members of "His Majesty's Council for Virginia." Another of her Vestrymen was George Mason, one of the first among the founders of the State and the great political thinkers of his age; while still another was declared to be the

INTRODUCTION

"Greatest man of any age," the imperial George Washington.

These men, however exalted their native genius, had and needed to have their period of training, that their characters might be matured on lines of piety and righteousness, their opinions formed in full view of the needs and capacities of their people, and their abilities ripened in the fields of practical experience. They received this training in part as Parish Vestrymen. It was no mean school in which to learn the rudiments of popular government, the foundations of human rights, or the reconciliation of diverse policies.

The Vestry Records of Truro Parish have therefore a value quite unique as the sole and absolutely authentic record of the parochial administration and government of these great men. The affairs which occupied their attention seem small indeed as compared with those which afterward demanded the consecration of their powers, but they brought to them the same practical wisdom, scrupulous justice and exact attention to detail which characterized them later as master workmen in making the history and building the liberties of a nation.

For the recovery and preservation of these records we are indebted to the late Reverend Doctor Philip Slaughter, Clergyman, Genealogist, Antiquarian and Historian, whose name will long be held in affectionate remembrance in Virginia. He was the author of no large work, but his his-

INTRODUCTION

tories of St. George's, Bristol, and St. Mark's Parishes, and very many pamphlets, articles and published addresses, combine to form a great contribution to the historical collections of his native State, and an enduring monument to his memory. A few years before his death he was so fortunate as to discover the whereabouts of the old Vestry-Book of Truro Parish which had been lost to sight for three-quarters of a century, and did not rest until it came into his possession. He afterwards committed it to the Vestry of Pohick Church, accepting only the small sum in return which it had cost him to acquire it, but not before he had compiled from its time-worn pages the History of Truro Parish which is here presented to the reader. It was almost his last literary labor, and indeed the infirmities of age forbade his giving the work of his amanuenses his final revision and corrections. The incomplete manuscript was entrusted to the Rev. Dr. Samuel A. Wallis, then Rector of Pohick, to be published when the means for doing so should be forthcoming.

At the request of Dr. Wallis I have prepared the history for publication. The manuscript has been wholly re-written; more copious extracts from the records of the Vestry have been incorporated, so that it now includes all that is of general value in the Vestry-Book, the language and spelling of which have been preserved; a few errors and oversights have been found and corrected; and in one

INTRODUCTION

place, for reasons noted in the text, a number of pages of my own have been inserted in lieu of the author's. With these exceptions the continuous narrative is as nearly as possible as Dr. Slaughter wrote it. My own additions otherwise appear in the form of foot-notes and addenda.

EDWARD L. GOODWIN.

The Rectory,

    Fairfax, Virginia.

THE GENESIS OF TRURO PARISH

Among the prominent features in the physiognomy of Eastern Virginia are the great rivers which run from the blue mountains and pour their streams into the bosom of the "Mother of Waters," as the Indians called the Chesapeake Bay. Along these rivers, which were then the only roads, the first settlers penetrated the wilderness. This explains the seeming anomaly, that the first Parishes and counties often included both sides of broad rivers, it being easier to go to Court and to Church by water, than through forests by what were called in those days "bridle paths." Hence Parishes were often sixty or more miles long and of little breadth. The space between the rivers was called "Necks." Among the most historic of these was the Northern Neck, which included all the land between the Potomac and the Rappahannock rivers from their head springs to the Chesapeake Bay. This was the princely plantation of Lord Fairfax. Within this territory were the seats of the Fairfaxes, Washingtons, Masons, McCartys, Fitzhughs, Brents, Alexanders, Lewises, Mercers, Daniels, Carters, Dades, Stuarts, Corbins, Tayloes, Steptoes, Newtons, Browns,

THE HISTORY OF TRURO PARISH

Lees, Thorntons, Balls, Smiths, and other leading families too many to mention, who dispensed an elegant hospitality at Northumberland House, Nomini, Stratford, Chantilly, Mount Airy, Sabine Hall, Bedford, Albion, Cedar Grove, Boscobel, Richland, Marleborough, Woodstock, Gunston, Belvoir, Woodlawn, Mount Vernon, etc. Beginning at Lancaster, county was taken from county, Parish from Parish, as the population of each passed the frontiers, until in 1730 Prince William was taken from Stafford and King George Counties, above Chappawansick Creek and Deep Run, and along the Potomac, to the "Great Mountains." This became also Hamilton Parish; which Parish, by an Act of the General Assembly passed at the Session of May, 1732, to take effect the first of the following November, was divided into two Parishes "By the river Ockoquan, and the Bull Run, (a branch thereof,) and a course from thence to the Indian Thoroughfare of the Blue Ridge of Mountains," (Ashby's Gap.) All that part of Prince William lying below the said bounds was to retain the name of Hamilton, "And all that other part of the said county, which lies above those bounds, shall hereafter be called and known by the name of Truro." The Parish was named after the Parish in Cornwall, in England, which is now the Diocese of Truro.

Such is the genesis of the Parish of Truro, which extended along the Potomac from the

THE HISTORY OF TRURO PARISH

mouth of Occoquan to the Blue Ridge, including what are now the Parishes of Truro, Cameron, Fairfax and Shelburne.* Within this territory there were three churches. Occoquan, William Gunnells, and a chapel "above Goose Creek."

The present writer has been so fortunate as to find the old Vestry Book of Truro Parish; so long lost to the public eye that even Bishop Meade said he could "hear no tidings" of it and was constrained to construct his sketch of the Parish from such facts and traditions as he could gather from other sources and from his own rich personal knowledge. It is now possible for the first time to authenticate its history by its own records, which are continuous from 1732 to 1785, when the civil functions of the Vestries were devolved by law upon the Overseers of the Poor. This book also contains a record of the proceedings of the Overseers of the Poor from 1787 to 1802, thus handing down the names of persons, many of whom had been Vestrymen of the Church.

The Vestry Book opens with a recitation of the Act of the General Assembly instituting the Parish, the election of the Vestry and the proceedings of their first meeting. The Act of Assembly prescribed that the Sheriff of the County should summon the freeholders and housekeepers to meet and elect so many of the "most able and discreet per-

---
*These are Colonial Parishes. Those of more recent foundation in the same territory are Johns, Upper Truro, McGill, and a part of Meade.

THE HISTORY OF TRURO PARISH

sons in the said Parish as shall make up the number of Vestrymen in the said Parish twelve and no more." Which order being complied with, "Five of the Vestrymen elected, to witt, Charles Broadwater, Richard Osborn, John Lewis, Gabriel Adams, and Edward Emms, together with Denis Mc.Carty, John Heryford, and Edward Barry, having taken the oaths appointed by law, and Subscribed to be conformable to the doctrine and discipline of the Church of England, took their places in the Vestry accordingly." The first Vestry met on November 7th, 1732, with the above gentlemen present. Edward Barry was nominated for Clerk, and "the question was put whether the said Barry should enjoy the place or not, which was carried in the said Barry's favour. And he was thereupon sworn, and took his place accordingly." He was ordered to "provide paper & books for the minutes and orders of this Vestry, and that he be paid for the same at the laying of the next parish levy." John Heryford and Edward Emms were chosen Churchwardens for that year, and "were sworn accordingly." At the next meeting of the Vestry, held March 26, 1733, John Sturman and Giles Tillett were added to the Vestry, and there were present also Francis Aubrey and William Godfrey, not previously mentioned. It was "Ordered, that the Churchwardens give publick notice to workmen to appear at the next Vestry to be held for this parish to agree for the building of a

THE HISTORY OF TRURO PARISH

Church at the cross roads near Michael Reagans in this parish." At the meeting on April 16, 1733, Michael Ashford took the oaths and subscribed the test as a Vestryman. An agreement was made with the Rev. Lawrence De Butts to preach three times a month for one year, "at Occoquan Church, the new Church, or William Gunnell's, and at the Chappell above Goose Creek,* for the sum of eight thousand pounds of tobacco clear of the Warehouse charges and abatements,—And the said De Butts doth further agree to and with the Vestry aforesaid, that in case he fails, or is by the weather prevented to preach at any of the places aforesaid, any of the times aforesaid, tobacco shall only be levied for him in proportion to his service." Mr. De Butts seems to have been a bird of passage. From 1721 to about 1728 he was Minister of Washington Parish in Westmoreland County, where he had two churches, and also officiated during the week in the neighboring Parishes of St.

---
*Occoquan Church, which Dr. Slaughter could not identify, was none other than the old Pohick Church, which stood about two miles from the ferry over the Occoquan at or near Colchester. When this Church was built is not known, but it was first an "Upper Church," or Chapel-of-Ease, in Overwharton Parish. When Hamilton Parish was formed, January 1, 1730, it was ordered that the freeholders and housekeepers meet "At the Church above Occoquan ferry" to elect their Vestry, "above" meaning up the Potomac. When Truro was set apart two years later this Church falls again in a new Parish. After the year 1733 the name Occoquan disappears and that of Pohick is substituted. The Church stood until superseded by the new or present Pohick in 1774.

"William Gunnell's Church" was probably a temporary, or perhaps a rented, building, and may have been situated not far below Difficult Run, as the Gunnells owned land in that vicinity. It disappears after the building of the "Church near Michael Reagan's," and may be considered the first Falls Church. The location of the "Chapel above Goose Creek" is not known. It was still unfinished at this time, being completed in 1736.

THE HISTORY OF TRURO PARISH

Stephen's, Northumberland; Farnham, Richmond County; and Cople, Westmoreland, when they were vacant. In 1731 he was employed in St. Mark's Parish, Culpepper County, at 500 pounds of tobacco a sermon, and now is in Truro for one year.* At the expiration of this engagement he seems to have preached eight sermons in the Parish, for which he received 245 pounds of tobacco per sermon, and then he disappears from the record, having, we believe, gone to Maryland.

1733, June 9th, Mr. Richard Blackburn agreed with the Vestry to build a Church at the Cross Roads near Michael Reagan's, "Forty feet in length, two and twenty feet wide, and thirteen feet pitch, to be weather boarded, covered, and all the inside work perform'd and done after the same manner the work upon Pohick Church is done, for the sum of thirty-three thousand five hundred pounds of tobacco." William Godfrey and Michael Ashford were "to take care that the work upon the Church be well and sufficiently done and performed."† 12th. October: Jeremiah Bronaugh,

---

*Paul Leicester Ford, in "The True George Washington," supposes that this Mr. De Butts officiated at the baptism of Washington. It is most improbable that such was the case. George Washington was born in Washington Parish, Westmoreland County, February 11th, 1731-2 (Old style,) and was baptized the third of April following, according to the record in the family Bible. Mr. De Butts had left Westmoreland several years before, and was now officiating in Truro Parish.

†This was known as the "Upper Church" until 1757, when the name "Falls Church" is first applied to it in the Vestry Book, probably to distinguish it more clearly from the Church in Alexandria. The Church was apparently built on land to which no title had been acquired, for in 1746 the Church Wardens were directed to pay John Trammel fifty shillings sterling for two acres of land at the Upper Church, and on the 19th of March of that year Trammel

THE HISTORY OF TRURO PARISH

William Peake, John Farguson and Thomas Lewis were chosen Vestrymen in the room of several deceased members, and qualified and took their places accordingly. Joseph Johnson was chosen "Reader at the new Church and the Chapell above Goose Creek," to receive 1300 pounds of tobacco "provided he does his duty in his office." In the Parish Levy for this year provision is made for 2500 pounds of tobacco to Capt. Francis Aubrey towards building the chapel above Goose Creek, and the next year the same amount, and in 1735, 4000 pounds for finishing said chapel.

1734, 11th. May; James Baxter was chosen a Vestryman and qualified. Ordered that Edward Emms, the upper Churchwarden, give notice to Capt. John Colvill to appear at a Vestry to be held at Pohick Church on the 4th. of June next, to take the oath of a Vestryman, if he shall think fit to accept of the office." Jeremiah Bronaugh, John Farguson and James Baxter were appointed to view the land offered for a Glebe by William Godfrey, French Mason, William Hall, George Harrison, and Burr Harrison, and any other land that shall be offered by any other person, and to report to the Vestry. On the 4th. of June John Colvill Gent. was sworn and took his seat as a Vestryman. There is a note on the margin here signed "C.

---
made them a deed, now on record at the Clerk's office at Fairfax, conveying two acres—"where the upper Church now is, to be laid off in such manner as the Vestry shall think proper, to include the said Church, churchyard and spring, and all appurtenances to the said premises."

THE HISTORY OF TRURO PARISH

G." (Rev. Charles Green,) in these words: "Capt. Colvill appears to have been a 13th Vestryman. This is noted because when a Burgess for this County he promoted ye dissolution of the Vestry as illegal,—himself the only illegal Vestryman." John Heryford offered to sell 300 acres of land, "Scituate, Lying and being upon Accotink, and near the plantation of David Jones," for a Glebe, for 12000 pounds of tobacco. It was ordered that the land be laid off at the cost of said Heryford, and that John Sturman provide Deeds of Lease and Release for conveying the land sold to this parish for a Glebe. The Churchwardens were ordered to receive of Wm. Godfrey 5000 pounds of tobacco he had assumed to pay to this parish for the parish of Hamilton.

"At a Vestry held for Truro Parish on the 23d. day of 7ber, 1734,—Whereas John Colvill Gent. one of the members of this Vestry, is in a short time bound for Great Brittain, and hath promised us that he will use his interest to procure a discreet and Godly Minister of the Church of England, to come over and settle in our said parish. And further that he will accommodate any such person with a free passage hither, on board any of his ships, if he is ready to come in any of them, and will accept of the same. We do therefore hereby impower and desire the said John Colvill to negotiate the said affair in our behalf, either by making application to his Grace the Lord Bishop

THE HISTORY OF TRURO PARISH

of London, or by treating with any gentleman qualified as aforesaid in his private capacity, who shall be willing to come over and settle here. And we do agree to accept of, and provide for him, in as full and ample manner as the law of this Colony directs." Signed by the Churchwardens and the five additional Vestrymen present.*

1734. Oct. 11th. After the expiration of the year for which the Rev. Mr. De Butts had been employed he seems to have preached occasionally in the Parish, for at a Vestry of this date provision was made for paying him 1970 pounds of tobacco "for preaching eight sermons." Payment was also ordered for Mr. Catesby Cocke for "Clerks Fees," to John Trammell for "grubing a place for the Church," to John Massey for "keeping a house for the minister to preach in," and to the Churchwardens "to buy tarr for the Churches." The salary of "each Reader in this parish" was fixed for the next year at 1000 pounds of tobacco.

1735. Nov. 18th. "Augustine Washington gent. being this day sworn one of the members of this Vestry, took his place therein accordingly." "C. G." interlines this note: "A. W. a fourteenth Vestryman, father to L. W. the other Burgess when Truro Vestry was dissolved."†

---

*Nothing more is found in the Vestry Book in regard to this effort to procure a minister from England. Doubtless it was fortunate for the Parish that the plan, for some reason, miscarried.
†Father also of George Washington, who inherited Mount Vernon from his brother, Lawrence Washington, the Burgess here indicated.

THE HISTORY OF TRURO, PARISH

Payment was ordered to Catesby Cocke, for recording deeds and copies of the lists of tithables in the Parish,* 168 pounds of tobacco; to Edward Barry, Clerk of the Church, (Pohick,) and Vestry, 1500 pounds; to Samuel Hull, Clerk of the Chapel above Goose Creek, and Joseph Johnson, Clerk of the new Church, 1000 pounds each, and to Oliver Roe, Sexton at Pohick, 300 pounds.

"At a Vestry held for Truro Parish the 19th. day of August, 1736,—Mr. Charles Green, being recommended to this Vestry by Capt. Augustine Washington as a person qualified to officiate as a Minister of this Parish as soon as he shall receive orders from his Grace the Bishop of London to qualify himself for the same. It is therefore ordered by this Vestry, that as soon as the said Green has qualified himself as aforesaid, he be received and entertained as Minister of the said Parish. And the said Vestry do humbly recommend the said Charles Green to the Right Honorable Thomas Lord Fairfax for his Letters of recommendation and Presentation to his Grace the said

---

*All male persons of the age of sixteen years or upwards, and also negro, mulatto and Indian women of like age, ("except tributary Indians to this government,") were "tithable" or chargeable for county and parish levies. But the Court or Vestry, "for reasons in charity," could excuse indigent persons from payment, and this was frequently done. In 1733 there were 676 tithables in Truro. Ten years later there were 1,372. This indicates the growth of the population. The Parish Levy varied widely year by year, the average being about 34 pounds of tobacco per poll.

THE HISTORY OF TRURO PARISH

Lord Bishop of London to qualify him as aforesaid.

Jeremiah Bronaugh, Church Warden.

Denis Mc.Carty	Willm. Godfrey
August. Washington	James Baxter
Richd. Osborn	Edward Barry
John Sturman	Thos. Lewis."

October 11th. The Vestry met and made the usual appropriations for the officers of the Church and for the support of the poor. They also made a bargain with the Rev. John Holmes to officiate in the Parish, in these words:—"Ordered that the Revd. Mr. John Holmes be received and entertained in this Parish, as Minister thereof; and that he be provided for as the Law directs." Further, it was "Ordered that the Reverend Mr. John Holmes Minister of this Parish preach six times in each year at the Chappell above Goose Creek; and it is also ordered, that the Sundays he preaches at the said Chappell the sermon shall be taken from the new Church." At the bottom of the page is the following note, signed Cha. Green;—"The Levity of the Members of the Vestry is worth notice, They applyed to Collo. Colvill & entered an order, 23d. Sept. 1734 for him to procure them a Clergyman from England. By the order on the other page they gave Cha. Green a title to the Psh. when ordained, and he had scarcely left the country when they received Mr. John Holmes into the parish as appears by the above order.

THE HISTORY OF TRURO PARISH

N. B. Mr. Holmes was an Itinerant Preacher without any orders, & recd. contrary to Law."

This note was made after Mr. Green became Rector of the Parish. The foregoing entries are the only evidence of the connection of Messrs. De Butts and Holmes with the Parish. These facts were unknown to Bishop Meade, who never saw this record. This book also reveals the fact that the Rev. James Keith, of Hamilton Parish, the Grandfather of Chief Justice Marshall, also officiated in this Parish, when it was without a minister. At this very Vestry an order was entered to pay the Rev. Mr. James Keith 10,544 pounds of tobacco for services rendered.

On the 12th of April, 1737, a long contract with minute specifications is recorded with William Berkeley for building a "Mansion house" on the Glebe, with kitchen, barn, dairy, meat house, and all other appurtenances to a well furnished country residence. The specifications as to the quality of the timber, the style of the work, etc., would be a suggestive and profitable study for modern Vestrymen. The cost of the buildings was to be 36,500 pounds of tobacco. Berkeley's bond, to Jeremiah Bronaugh and Thomas Lewis, Church Wardens, with Lewis Ellzey, Hugh West, George Harrison, and John Minor as bondsmen, and Val. Peyton, Abraham Saintclare and Joseph Cash as witnesses, is also recorded in the Vestry Book. At the same time an agreement was made with John

THE HISTORY OF TRURO PARISH

Summers to "pale in the yard about the new Church after the same manner the yard about the Church at Pohick is paled in, (only the pails to be sawed,) to make good and sufficient shutters for the windows of the said Church, and to make and erect two good and substantial horse blocks," for 3000 pounds of tobacco.

THE REV. CHARLES GREEN, M. D.,
THE FIRST REGULAR RECTOR
OF TRURO PARISH.

The Vestry which met on the 13th of August, 1737, was the first which was held under the auspices of a regular Rector, and the following proceedings were entered on the minutes:

"Whereas at a Vestry held for this Parish on the nineteenth day of August one thousand seven hundred and thirty six, the now Reverend Mr. Charles Green was recommended to the Right Honorable Thomas Lord Fairfax, for his presentation of the said Green to the Lord Bishop of London for his ordination. And it now appearing to this Vestry, as well by the letter of the Honorable William Gooch Esqr. Lieutenant Governor of Virginia, as the letter of the Reverend Mr. James Blair Commissary, that the said Green is regularly and legally ordained. It is therefore ordered by this Vestry, that the said Green be received into, and entertained as Minister of, this

THE HISTORY OF TRURO PARISH

parish; and that he be provided for, as the laws of this Colony direct."*

This being passed there is noted as "Present, the reverend Mr. Charles Green Minister."

"Ordered, that the Church Wardens place the people that are not already placed, in Pohick and the new Churches, in pews, according to their several ranks and degrees."

"Ordered, that the sum of two thousand five hundred pounds of tobacco be yearly levied for the Reverend Mr. Charles Green, until the buildings that are to be erected upon the Glebe be compleated according to agreement made with the undertaker."

"Ordered, that the Reverend Mr. Charles Green preach four times in a year only, at the Chappell above Goose Crek. And that the Sunday he preaches at the said Chappell, the sermon shall be taken from the new Church."

At a Vestry on the third day of October, 1737, the usual appropriations for the salaries of the minister and other officers of the Church, and for the poor and other current expenses of the Parish,

---

*The Rev. Mr. Green was a Doctor of Medicine before he took orders, and appears to have practised to some extent afterwards. On at least one occasion he was called in at Mount Vernon, for lack of a regular practitioner, and prescribed for the relief of Mrs. Washington. He was a large landowner, and his Deeds, in which he is described as Doctor of Physic and Clerk of Truro Parish, are of frequent occurrence in the land records of the County. In his latter years his health appears to have been poor. In his will, probated August 19th, 1765, he leaves 3,000 acres of land, lying in Fairfax, Prince William and Loudoun, to his wife. He also mentions certain relatives in Ireland, and advises his wife to return to that country, from which it is supposed that he was an Irishman.

THE HISTORY OF TRURO PARISH

were made, amounting to 38,383 pounds of tobacco. The Parish Levy was at the rate of 42½ pounds per Poll. The next year it was 45 pounds. Among the appropriations made were;

To the Rev. Charles Green, Minister, salary,*	16729	lbs.	tobacco.
To Mr. Joseph Blumfield,† to be paid Rev. Chas. Green. .	1597	"	"
To Edward Washington, Sub Sheriff, per account.	300	"	"
To Francis Aubrey gent. for finding books for the Chappell	200	"	"
To buy ornaments for the Churches and books for the Chappell, and Plate for Communion	8000	"	"
To Mr. Richard Osborn for taring the Churches, &c. . . .	1100	"	"
To Edward Emms for *salivating* James Boilstone. . . .	1000	"	"

The Readers at the churches received their usual 1000 pounds, and the Sextons 500. A com-

---
*The Ministers salary was fixed by the law of 1696 at 16,000 pounds of tobacco. In 1727 the "cask" was added, for which an addition of eight per cent. was allowed; though for some reason in Truro only four per cent. was added for cask, and Mr. Green's salary after this time was 16,640 pounds, until in 1748 an additional four per cent. was allowed for "shrinkage." Thereafter the salary was 17,280 pounds, with, of course, the Glebe and buildings demanded by law. The value of a Minister's "Living" depended not a little on the quality of the tobacco raised in his Parish. Commissary Blair used to distinguish between "Sweet-scented" and "Oronoco" Parishes.

†The Rev. Mr. Blumfield, who seems to have performed occasional ministerial services in the parish before the arrival of Mr. Green.

THE HISTORY OF TRURO PARISH

mission of 6 per cent. was paid for collecting the levy.

"Whereas the Rev. Charles Green hath this day agreed with the Vestry to take the tobacco levied to purchase books for the Chappell above Goose Creek and ornaments for the Churches, at the rate of eleven shillings current money per hundred. He by the said agreement obliging himself to find and provide the said books and ornaments, being allowed fifty per cent. upon the first cost in accounting with the Church Wardens. It is ordered that the collector pay to the said Green the sum of 8000 pounds of tobacco, it being the quantity this day levied for the purpose aforesaid." Mr. Green also contracted to build the addition to the Glebe house for the sum appropriated.

Among the offices of the Church Wardens was the duty of binding orphan and other indigent children as Apprentices; and ten pages of the Vestry Book at this period are filled with Indentures. Their specifications in regard to the duties and morals of those apprenticed, their being taught to read English and the "Art and mystery" of shoemaking, or of a Carpenter, or Cooper, etc., are curious illustrations of the times.

At a Vestry held 6th. of October, 1740, a petition was presented from William Fairfax Esqr. Catesby Cocke, Gent. and Charles Green, Doctor of Physick, "setting forth that the Church at Pohick is too small to admit of a commodious re-

THE HISTORY OF TRURO PARISH

ception for the parishioners who resort to divine services at the said Church, and praying that they may be admitted to build a Gallery at the West end of the said Church for the reception and more easie accommodation of themselves and their families, and that the same may be erected at their own proper cost. It is ordered that they may have liberty to erect the same, so that it does discommode the lights of the Church, or interfere with any other conveniency thereto belonging."

"Col. John Colvill is appointed and chosen Church Warden in the room of Thomas Lewis."

In 1741 nothing appears on the record but the ordinary routine of laying levies, and making annual appropriations for the poor, and the other current expenses of the Parish.

INSTITUTION OF FAIRFAX COUNTY

In 1742 Fairfax County was taken from Prince William, and the boundary lines of Truro Parish and of the new county coincided.*

---

*The Act forming the new County, "Consisting of the Parish of Truro," (including what are now Loudoun and Alexandria Counties, as well as Fairfax,) took effect December 1st, 1742. (Hening, V, 207.) The first Court-House was established on "Freedom Hill," a mile or two north of the present village of Vienna, on land deeded to the County by William Fairfax. Probably that was then near the center of population. In 1754 the Court-House was moved to Alexandria, and on July 1st, 1757, Loudoun County was cut off from Fairfax. An Act of Assembly was passed December 4, 1789, directing two acres of land to be purchased and the county buildings to be erected "Within one mile of the cross roads, near Price's Ordinary," that being near the center of the County. But it was not until 1801 that the present Court-House was completed, on land deeded by Richard Ratcliffe, and the Court removed. The village which slowly grew up at the County seat received the name of

THE HISTORY OF TRURO PARISH

Among the duties of the Vestries was the appointment every four years of reputable Freeholders to "perambulate" the Parish,—going around the plantations and renewing the landmarks. This was called "Processioning."* To this end the Parish was divided into precincts, like our modern Townships. These are reproduced because they throw light upon the geography and population of the precincts at the time of the several processionings, and also because the Processioners named owned land within their several precincts at that date, and their names and localities are thus prescribed.

At a Vestry held the 8th of August, 1743, for appointing Processioners, etc. "Pursuant to an order of Fairfax County Court the Vestry proceeded and laid off the said Parish into precincts and appointed Processioners in manner following:

"Ordered, that Richard Simpson and Thos. Ford procession all the pattented lands that lye

---

Providence, while the County seat of Culpeper County was known as Fairfax. The old Virginia habit of calling the County seat "The Court-House" prevailed, however, and both villages lost their names, until finally, aided by the mandate of the Post Office Department, "Culpeper Court-House" became "Culpeper" and "Fairfax Court-House" has now become "Fairfax."

*This was a revival in Virginia, in about the year 1662, of an old English and Scottish custom which had already fallen into disuse in the old country. Processionings were required every four years. Originally the Vestries had only to mark out the precincts, and appoint the days, between Easter and Whitsunday, for the processioning, which was performed by the parties interested, but after 1705 they had also to "appoint at least two intelligent honest freeholders of each precinct to see such processioning performed, to take and return to the Vestry an account of every persons land they shall procession, and of the persons present at the same." These accounts were to be carefully recorded and preserved by the Vestry in books specially provided. Three processionings fixed the bounds of lands beyond dispute.

THE HISTORY OF TRURO PARISH

between Occoquan and Pohick on the upper side of the Ox road, and between that and Occoquan as far up as Popes head. and that they perform the same sometime in the month of October or November next, and report their proceedings according to Law." In like manner it was ordered, that William Champneys and Francis Cofer procession between Occoquan and Pohick, and on the lower side of the Ox road, as far up as the head branches of Popes head; that John Manley and John Brown procession between Pohick and Doegs Creek, from the head branches of Pohick by Col. Fitzhughs Rolling road, to the head of Doegs Run; that Zephaniah Wade and Sampson Darrell procession between Doegs Run and Great Hunting Creek; that Daniel French Senior and John Gladdin procession between Great Hunting Creek and Pimmetts Run; that James Robertson and Guy Broadwater procession between Pimmetts Run and Difficult Run; that John Trammell and John Harle procession between Difficult Run and Broad Run; that Anthony Hampton and William Moore procession between Broad Run and the south side of Goose Creek as far as the fork of Little River; that Philip Noland and John Lasswell procession between Goose Creek and Limestone Run as far as the fork of Little River; that Amos Janney and William Halling procession between Limestone Run and the south branch of Kitoctan; "Between the south fork of Kitoctan and Williams Gap, no

THE HISTORY OF TRURO PARISH

freeholder in this precinct. Between Williams Gap, Ashbys Gap, the county line, and Goose Creek, to the Beaver Dam, and back to the Gap. No freeholder in this precinct. Between the Beaver Dam and the north east fork of Goose Creek. No freeholder in this precinct."—that Lovel Jackson and Jacob Lasswell procession between the north east and north west forks of Goose Creek; that John Middleton and Edward Hews procession between Little River and Goose Creek; that William West and William Hall Junior procession between Little River and Walnut Cabbin branch; that George Adams and Daniel Diskin procession between Walnut Cabbin branch, Broad run and Cub run; that William Berkley and Vincent Lewis procession between Cub run and Popes head. "Ordered, that the Processioners, according to their judgement, shape a line from the head of one branch to the head of another; and that if any persons land crosses any of the natural boundarys mentioned, the first set of Processioners are to go round the land."

Vestry Dissolved, and a New Vestry Elected

In 1744 it was represented to the General Assembly that divers members of the Vestry of Truro Parish were not able to read or write, and were not otherwise qualified. The Vestry was dissolved

THE HISTORY OF TRURO PARISH

by an Act of Assembly, and the Sheriff of the County was ordered to call a meeting of the freeholders and housekeepers to choose a new Vestry of the "most able and discreet persons in the Parish." In obedience to this order the following persons were chosen to compose the new Vestry, viz:

Capt. John West   Capt. Richard Osborn
Capt. Lewis Ellzey   Mr. Daniel French
Mr. John Sturman   Mr. Edward Emms
Capt. John Minor   Mr. Robert Boggess
Mr. Hugh West   Colo. John Colvill
Mr. Andrew Hutchinson Mr. Charles Broadwater.

These persons, having taken the oaths required by law to be taken, subscribed the test, and to be conformable to Doctrine and Discipline of the Church of England, were sworn Vestrymen of the Parish of Truro.*

Bishop Meade expresses surprise at this dissolution in view of the number of intelligent men in the Parish, and supposes that it must have taken place elsewhere. But the Rev. Charles Green made a note in the Vestry Book which explains the proceeding. He says that "One of the causes assigned for the dissolution of the Vestry was that

---

*These political oaths were three in number, and the third was quite long. They were oaths of allegiance and of abjuration of Popery and of the Pretender, etc., and were required of all Civil and Military officers by the laws of England and of Virginia. They may be seen in Bp. Meade's "Old Churches, Ministers and Families of Virginia," Vol. II, p. 41. It seems to have required as many as six oaths and subscriptions properly to qualify a Vestryman in those days.

THE HISTORY OF TRURO PARISH

several of them were illiterate. There was but one of them illiterate, namely Edward Emms, who was reelected." The truth seems to be that the Delegates to the Assembly and other leading men often had Vestries dissolved when they displeased them.*

John West and Lewis Ellzey were sworn as Church Wardens, and William Henry Terrett was elected Clerk of the Vestry.

1745, April 15th. Messrs. John West, Hugh West, Hutchinson, French, Boggess and Broadwater were appointed to "view the most convenient place between Sailsbury plain, Little river and Potomac river for a Chappel of Ease to be built, and to treat with the workmen about the building thereof," and report to the Vestry.† Also

---

*The Act of Dissolving the Vestry of Truro was proposed in the House of Burgesses by Lawrence Washington, Esq., Oct. 15, 1744. It will be found in Hening's Statutes, Vol. V, p. 274. The preamble states that "many of them were never lawfully chosen or qualified; that several are not able to read or write." While the charge of illiteracy was doubtless overstated there can be no doubt that some of the Vestrymen were not lawfully chosen; for while the law was very explicit in limiting the number of Vestrymen in a parish to twelve, there were at least sixteen at one time in Truro, and on three occasions thirteen were recorded as being present at a Vestry.

By an Act of Assembly in 1745 the election of the new Vestry was confirmed, and the said Vestry was established as the legal Vestry of the Parish. Hening, Vol. V, p. 380.

†This Church was not built by the Truro Vestry. On October 7th of this same year it was "Ordered, that the Church to be built be built at Rocky run instead of the place already appointed, it appearing there is no water there, and that the Clerk prepare deeds for Capt. Newton to sign and execute for land for the use of the Church." After this we hear nothing more of it in the Vestry Book, and no tobaccoo was levied in this Parish for its erection. The site selected fell in Cameron Parish upon the division in 1749, and that the Church was built immediately thereafter we discover from a fragment of the records of the County Court of Fairfax for that period which escaped destruction. On July 21, 1752, the Court ordered "That Lewis Ellzey, Hugh West jr. James Hamilton, Demsie Cairde and James Halley, or any three of them, view and mark a way for a road to be cleared the most convenient way from

THE HISTORY OF TRURO PARISH

ordered that Messrs. John West, Ellzey and French view what necessary repairs are wanting at Goose Creek Chapel and agree with workmen therefor; that a gallery be built in the west end of the upper Church and the Church Wardens agree with workmen for the same; and that the Minister make choice of proper persons to officiate as Readers at each Church. May 21st it was ordered "That a Church be built at or near the spring nigh Mr. Hutchinsons and the Mountain road," 40 feet long, 22 feet wide and 13 feet pitch, weatherboarded, shingled, and "ceiled with quartered plank beaded and plained,—with pulpit, desk, Communion Table, pews, doors, windows and seats after the manner of the upper Church." The Clerk was instructed to prepare deeds for Mr. Hutchinson's conveyance of two acres of land for the Church and churchyard, and articles of agreement and bond for Hugh Thomas, who undertakes to build the Church for 24,500 pounds of tobacco, to be finished by the end of October 1746. On October 14th, 1746, John Summers, William Harle and Thomas Darus were appointed "to view the new Church, and to report on oath the state

---

Alexandria to Rocky Run Chappell, and report to the Court." On November 21st the same parties were sworn and ordered to open the road. Doubtless this is what is now locally known as the old Braddocks Road; and if a part of Gen. Braddock's force did pass over it in the spring of 1755 they may have found it in such an unfinished condition as to compel them to do further work on it, so giving rise to the tradition that it was opened by Braddock. The site of the Chapel would seem to have been at or near the point where this road crosses Little Rocky Run, about half a mile east of Centerville.

and condition of the work, whether there is an deficiency or not." Also it was "Ordered, that the Minister preach eight times in the year at the New Church, and that he do proportion the times equally from each Church."*

The following items from the accounts current show the payments to the officers of the Churches, etc.:

Rev. Charles Green, Salary and cask	16,640	lbs. of tobacco	
Clerks at Pohick, Upper Church, New Church, and Goose Creek, each	1200	"	"
Clerk of the Vestry	500	"	"
Mary Bennit, Sexton at the Upper Church	400	"	"
Do. for washing the surplice	125	"	"
Philip Howel, Sexton at Pohick, and washing surplice twice	550	"	"
Hugh West, for account book	110	"	"
Do. for bringing said book from Williamsburg	50	"	"

---

*This Church was probably located near the present village of Dranesville. The deed from Hutchinson to the Vestry is on record in the Clerk's Office of Fairfax, dated August 19th, 1745. He conveys two acres, near the Mountain road, to be laid off at the expense of the Parish, so as to include the Church intended and agreed to be built thereon, with a spring, etc. On the division of the Parish this Church fell in Cameron.

THE HISTORY OF TRURO PARISH

Dr. Robinson, physick and attendance on poor......	1200	"	"
Dr. Daniel Hart, per account, for poor.........	3880	"	"
Various items, relief of the poor, one year..........	4630	"	"

A Mandamus

In the proceedings of the Vestry for June, 1747, it is said that a Mandamus was presented to the Vestry in behalf of William Grove; who being examined denied that he knew anything of its being prosecuted, and also quit all claim to the Clerk's place. This is the first instance of a Mandamus being served on a Vestry that I have met with. It is explained by a note on the margin by the Minister, thus: "William Grove was recommended to me by Capt. Newton as a person capable to be Clerk Etc. but on trial was found not capable. Also he came into the County convicted, though probably he might have behaved well afterward. For these reasons I appointed Wm. Champneys Clerk, which occasioned the Mandamus."

William Grove was made *Sexton* at the new Church.

In 1748, in addition to the usual items, payments were made to John Graham, Valentine Wade, Mary Willis, Baldwin Dade, John Carlyle,

THE HISTORY OF TRURO PARISH

and William Moore for levies overcharged, and to Dr. John Hunter for services to the poor.

First Division of Truro Parish

By an act of the Assembly of October, 1748, it was enacted that from and after the eleventh day of June then next Truro Parish should be divided, "by Difficult Run and its meanders from the mouth to the head thereof, thence by a line to the head of Popes head run, and down the said run to the mouth thereof." All on the lower side of said runs and line to retain the name of Truro, and all on the upper side to be "one other distinct Parish and called by the name of Cameron."*

Truro was now limited to the foregoing metes and bounds; and Cameron Parish had jurisdiction above the said line, with its own Minister and Vestry. The division transferred 707 tithables to Cameron, leaving 1240 in Truro. Several of the

---

*See Hening's Statutes, Vol. VI, pp. 214 and 271. In 1757 Fairfax County was divided and Loudoun County formed, the line being as follows: "Difficult run, which falls into Patowmack river, and a line to be run from the head of the said run, a straight course, to the mouth of Rocky run;" (Now known as Little Rocky Run, emptying into the Bull Run.) This left a small part of Cameron Parish, lying between Popes Head and the above line, still in Fairfax. By another Act, however, in effect January 1st, 1763, this was taken from Cameron and added to Truro, so that the parish and County lines should coincide. (See Hening, Vol. VII, pp. 148 and 612.) In 1798 the present line between Fairfax and Loudoun was established, being about eight miles west of the old line; but of course at that date no change was made in the Parish lines by the Legislature, and Cameron again lay partly in Fairfax. This fact was forgotten, however, and when in 1884 a new Parish was formed, almost entirely within the territory of Cameron, it received the name of Upper Truro Parish.

THE HISTORY OF TRURO PARISH

old Vestrymen also lived in Cameron. The new Vestry of Truro consisted of,—

Hugh West,   Abraham Barnes,
George Mason,   Thomas Wren,
James Hamilton,   Robert Boggess
Charles Broadwater,   John Turley,
Daniel Mc.Carty,   William Peake,
William Payne,   Jeremiah Bronaugh.

This is the first appearance of the great Author of the Bill of Rights in the Vestry Book. Mr. Bronaugh died within a few months, and was succeeded as Church Warden by Mr. Mason and as Vestryman by John West.*

February 19, 1749-50, the Vestry agree with Charles Broadwater Gent. to make an addition to the Upper Church, according to plans produced, for 12,000 pounds of tobacco. It was also ordered that the sills and sleepers of Pohick Church be repaired, the north side of the Church newly shingled with poplar or chestnut shingles, that windows be made in the "Justices Pew" and in the "Womens Pew," that the Church be raised and new blocked, and that a Vestry House be built, sixteen feet square, framed and clapboarded, to have "an inside wooden chimney and to be lofted with clapboards." Capt. Daniel McCarty undertakes this work for 5,500 pounds of tobacco, he

---

*This was the third Vestry of Truro. We miss henceforward several familiar names, among them our old friends, Edward Emms, Richard Osborn and Andrew Hutchinson. It is very likely that two at least of these would be found on the first Vestry of Cameron.

THE HISTORY OF TRURO PARISH

having also the material in the old Vestry House to make what use of he can in building the new. Afterward this work was ordered to be deferred, and two years later the contract, with the addition of a window by the pulpit and making good the pews and floor, was given to Mr. Daniel French for sixty-three pounds current money.

On the 20th of May, 1751, it was ordered, "That the Clerk of the Vestry present unto the next Court of Claims and Propositions a petition in the name of the Minister, Churchwardens and Vestry of this Parish to Honour'l. House of Burgesses setting forth the insufficiency and inconveniency of the Glebe land of said Parish in order that an Act of Assembly be obtained for the Vestry to sell the same and buy land more convenient for the same uses, and also to pay the upper Parish of this County their proportion of what the said land may sell for."* In 1752 an Act of Assembly granted the petition.

The time for processioning the lands having come again, and the division of the Parish having changed its geography, etc. It was ordered that James Donaldson and John Jenkins procession between Difficult and Pimmetts run, Guy Broadwater and James Robertson between Pimmetts

---
*From the County Court records, February 8th, 1752. "A petition for selling the Glebe lands in the Parish of Truro and purchasing other land more convenient presented and ordered certified to the Assembly."
For the Act see Hening, VI, 270. It is from this Act that we discover the lines between Truro and Cameron, the Act providing for the division being lost except its title.

THE HISTORY OF TRURO PARISH

run and Four Mile run, Edward Masterson and William Gleading between Four Mile run and Hunting Creek, Sampson Darrell and John Posey between Hunting Creek and Dogue run, Edward Violet and William Ashford between Dogue run and Accotink, Abraham Barnes and Robert Boggess between Accotink and Pohick, William Reardon and John Hereford between Pohick and Occoquan to Sandy run, Thomas Ford and Richard Simpson from Sandy run to Popes Head and the branches of Difficult.

1752. The Glebe was sold at auction and bought by Mr. William Ramsay for fifty pounds current money; and 176 acres of land adjoining the old Glebe was bought of Rev. Charles Green for 13,500 pounds of tobacco. Proposals were invited for buildings on the Glebe according to law, the dwelling house to be of brick, to contain in the clear about 1200 feet, of one story and a cellar and convenient rooms and closets; to be advertised in the Gazette and at the several Churches and the Courthouse. In October Mr. Thomas Waite contracted for the dwelling house and other houses on the Glebe for 425 pounds current money, and Rev. Charles Green undertook to do the rest of the building necessary, apparently without compensation.

The Clerk of the Upper Church was directed to "read prayers every intervening Sunday," and was allowed 1200 pounds of tobacco for his salary.

THE HISTORY OF TRURO PARISH

ALEXANDRIA

1753, June 4th. "On the petition of Capt. John West ordered that the Rev. Mr. Charles Green do preach every third Sunday at the Town of Alexandria." This is the first time Alexandria is mentioned in this record, and this is probably the date of the first Chlrch services there. Hitherto it has not been supposed that there had been Church service at Alexandria before 1762. It is not generally known that the site of Alexandria was included in a grant of land, (6,000 acres,) extending from Hunting Creek to the Little Falls, from Sir William Berkeley to Robert Howson. In October, 1669, Howson, for six hogsheads of tobacco, conveyed these lands to John Alexander, who, with his brothers Robert and Gerard, had emigrated from Scotland. (See Dinwiddie Papers, Vol. I, p. 89.) There had been for some years warehouses at Pohick, Hunting Creek, and at Thomas Lee's land at the Falls, when, in 1748, a town named Alexandria was established by Act of Assembly at Hunting Creek Warehouse, sometimes called Belle-Haven.

In 1754 there is mention of the payment of 100 pounds of tobacco to Capt. John West for "part of building the desk at Alexandria." And in 1756 the Churchwardens are ordered "to have seats made for the Church at Alexandria."*

---

*Strange to say these are the only mentions made in this Vestry Book of any levy or appropriation for building, furnishing or

THE HISTORY OF TRURO PARISH

Colchester

As Colchester was a conspicuous feature of Truro Parish it may be well to record here that it was established as a Town by Act of Assembly in 1753-4 on 25 acres of land belonging to Peter Wagener, as being "very convenient for trade, and greatly to the ease of frontier inhabitants." The Trustees and Directors were Peter Wagener, Daniel McCarty, John Barry, William Ellzey, and Edward Washington, all Vestrymen of Truro Parish.

1754. Messrs. George Mason, Daniel McCarty, and Hugh West, who had been appointed to view the buildings on the Glebe as they progressed, made a report, showing the manliness of the times, which some modern Vestries would do well to imitate. They say the bricks are not fit to be used, and that the following notice should be given to Mr. Waite, the undertaker, and his securities:—
"Mr. Waite: The Vestry are of opinion that none of the bricks of the two first kilns are fit to be put into the walls of the Glebe House, but that what is done be pulled down and done with good bricks and that the cellar windows be done with good ring oak or locust; and that in case you begin anew that they will allow you six months further

---

repairing a Church in Alexandria; though hereafter the Clerk and the Sexton at Alexandria are regularly paid as at the other Churches. It is probable therefore that Capt. West and others themselves provided a hall or Chapel for services, even paying in part for building the desk.

THE HISTORY OF TRURO PARISH

than the time mentioned in your bond to compleat it."

"Ordered, that the King's Attorney do prosecute for this Parish."

The Hon. William Fairfax was appointed Vestryman in the room of Hugh West, deceased. The Churchwardens were directed to give notice for the impotent people of the Parish to appear before the Vestry the following May, and also any person who will undertake to board them.

September, 1755. The time for processioning land recurs, and some of the details are given because they throw light on the history of the Parish. David Piper, John Hereford, and Marielles Littlejohn are to procession the several tracts of land that have their beginnings between Occoquan, Potomac river, Accotink run and the road that leads from Hunting Creek through the Glebe land to Occoquan. John Peak, Daniel French, John Posey, and Abednego Adams, between Accotink, Potomac river, Hunting Creek and the road that leads from Hunting Creek through the Glebe land. John Dalton, Thomas Harrison, John Hunter, and Nathaniel Smith, between Hunting Creek, Potomac river, and the road that leads from Awbreys ferry to the upper Church and the road that leads from Cameron to the said Church. Guy Broadwater, James Robertson and James Donaldson, between the road that leads from Awbreys ferry to the upper Church and the road from up-

THE HISTORY OF TRURO PARISH

per Church to Difficult run, and then down the run to Potomac river, and then down the river to Awbreys ferry. Lewis Ellzey, James Hawley, William Adams, and John Ratcliff, between the road that leads from Cameron to Difficult run, and up the run and Parish line till the line comes to the road that leads from Cameron by Capt. Lewis Ellzeys, and so down the said road to Cameron. Thomas Shaw, Presley Cox, James Jugo Dozier, Joseph Stephens, Sampson Demevill, and John Hampton between the road that leads from Cameron by Capt. Lewis Ellzeys to the Parish line, and so down the Parish line to Occoquan ferry, and then up the road by the Glebe to Hunting Creek.

Mrs. Sybil West is paid 1800 pounds of tobacco for elements for the Churches. Wm. Payne and Henry Gunnell chosen Vestrymen in 1756.

1757. Geo. Wm. Fairfax chosen Vestryman in the room of his father, Hon. William Fairfax, deceased.* Several parties were paid for attendance as witnesses in Churchwardens suit against Cole.

1758. John West jun. becomes Clerk of the Vestry. George Mason, John West and Daniel

---

*William Fairfax was a cousin of Thomas, Lord Fairfax, Proprietor of the Northern Neck, and his agent in Virginia until he himself came over. He was a Burgess from Prince William Co. from 1742 until 1744, when he became a member of the Governor's Council. George William Fairfax was a Burgess from Frederick Co. from 1752 to 1755, and from Fairfax, 1756-58. He also became a member of the Council in 1768. He was a half brother of the Rev. Bryan, Lord Fairfax, afterward Rector of Christ Church, Alexandria.

THE HISTORY OF TRURO PARISH

McCarty to examine the Parish papers and report to the next Vestry.

1759. Mr. Waite, "tho' often admonished," having failed in doing his work at the Glebe buildings according to agreement, the Vestry take steps to annul his contract. William Bucklands finally completes the work and is paid the balance due Waite. Processioners were again appointed, being generally those who had served before.

1760 and 1761. We have only the usual routine Parish items and appropriations for salaries, maintenance of the poor, Physicians and Lawyers fees, etc. Mrs. Sybil West's account for elements for the Holy Communion is about 1100 pounds of tobacco annually.

George Washington, Vestryman

1762. October 25th. "Ordered, that George Washington Esqr. be chosen and appointed one of the Vestrymen of this Parish in the room of William Peake Gent. deceased."*

The Falls Church

"At a Vestry held at the Falls Church March 28th, 1763. Present, Henry Gunnell, William Payne jun. Church Wardens, John West, William Payne (sen.) Chas. Broadwater, Thos. Wren,

---

*From the Records of the County Court of Fairfax, February 15th, 1763: "George Washington Esqr. took the oaths according to Law repeated and subscribed the Test and subscribed to the Doctrine and Discipline of the Church of England in order to qualify him to act as a Vestryman of Truro Parish."

above the foundations with Brick or Tile floor covered with cypress shingles, Ceiling and Walls Plaistered and whitewashed, One pannell'd Door in the broadside with a Sash Window with twelve Lights and pannel Shutters opposite, Barge boards and Cornice, The Door, Window and Shutters, Barge Boards & Cornice to be painted, a Lock to the Door, and the whole to be finished in a Workman like manner by Christmass next — The said House to be furnished with a Table and three Benches for making, which and the Cornice, they undertake to be allowed a Sufficiency of Plank out of the Parishes Plank now in Samuel Littlejohns Tobacco House — And Cap't Edward Payne having undertaken and agreed with this Vestry to build the said House in manner aforesaid & by the times above mentioned, and to provide the said Table and three Benches for the Sum of Fifty one pounds Ten Shillings Cur't Money, one half to be paid by the first day of August next, and the Remainder on or before the first day of August 1768 — Ordered that the same be paid him accordingly. —

G: Washington } C:W
William Gardner }

G Mason
Edw'd Payne
Jn'o Posey
Daniel McCarty
Alex'r Henderson
Tho's Withers Coffer
William Linton
Thomason Ellzey

Truely Record
Test John Burgiss Cl'k Vestry

The Old Vestry Book

At a Vestry held for Truro Parish, this 22d Day
May 17th of the Feb'y:
 Present The Rev'd Lee Massey Minister
Mess'rs George Washington & W'm Gardner Church Wardens
 George Mason   John Posey
 Edw'd Payne   Vestrymen
 Dan'l McCarty   W'm Linton

Mr. Thomisson Ellzey having returned a Plott of a
Survey made of the Glebe Land, pursuant to a former
order of Vestry, containing three hundred eighty
five Acres and an half only, which said Quantity
of Land being exposed to Sale to the highest Bidder
was purchased by Daniel McCarty Gent. at the Rate
of Three hundred and twenty two pounds, Virginia
Currency, Who gave his Bond with Mr. Richard
Chichester his Security for the same, payable
eighteen Months hence, to George Washington and
William Gardner Churchwardens, for the Use of
this Parish.

The Church Plate being also exposed to sale
was purchased by the said Daniel McCarty at the
Price of Twenty Six pounds, Virginia Currency for
the Use of the Parish —

 Lee Massey
 G: Washington ⎱ Ch. Wardens
 W'm Gardner ⎰
 G: Mason
 Edw'd Payne
 Jn'o Posey
Truly Recorded Dan'l McCarty
 Test, & William Linton
 John Barry Clk Vestry

THE HISTORY OF TRURO PARISH

Abra. Barnes, Danl. Mc.Carty, Robt. Boggess, and Geo. Washington, Vestrymen, Who being there met to examine into the state of the said Church, greatly in decay and want of repairs, and likewise whether the same should be repaired or a new one built, and whether at the same place or removed to a more convenient one;—Resolved it is the opinion of this Vestry that the old Church is rotten and unfit for repair, but that a new Church be built at the same place. Ordered that the Clerk of the Vestry advertise in the Virginia and Maryland Gazettes for workmen to meet at the said Church on the 29th day of August next, if fair, if not the first fair day, to undertake the building a Brick Church to contain 1600 feet on the floor, with a suitable gallery, and bring a plan for the Church and price according to the same."

There is no record of a meeting in August. Probably no contractors appeared.

October 3rd. 1763. "Ordered, that George William Fairfax and George Washington Esqrs. be appointed Church Wardens for the ensuing year."

"Ordered, that the Vestry meet at Alexandria on the third Tuesday in March next in order to agree with workmen to undertake the building a Church at or near the old Falls Church, and that the Church Wardens advertise the same in the Virginia and Maryland Gazettes to be continued six weeks; and that it will be then expected of each

THE HISTORY OF TRURO PARISH

workmen to produce a plan and estimate of the expense." The Parish Levy called for 30,000 pounds of tobacco" towards building the Falls Church, to be sold for cash by the Church Wardens for the highest price they can get." Again there is no record of the meeting appointed for March (1764) being held.* But in the annual Levy laid in October of that year an additional 20,000 pounds of tobacco is levied "for building Churches in the Parish," and ordered to be sold as before. John Barry becomes Clerk of the Vestry.

SECOND DIVISION OF TRURO, AND FORMATION OF FAIRFAX PARISH

[Note by the Editor.—The facts in regard to the division of Truro, and the formation of Fairfax Parish, are not recorded in the Vestry

---

*Perhaps the Church Wardens overlooked their charge to advertise for contractors until after this Vestry was to have met. But on May 17th, 1764, their advertisement appeared in the Maryland Gazette, a copy of which is preserved in the Library of Congress, and ran for six weeks, as follows:
"Virginia, Fairfax county, March 20, 1764.
Notice is hereby given to any Person or Persons, who are willing to undertake the Building a Brick Church at the Falls in Truro Parish in the County aforesaid, (to contain 1600 feet superficial Measure, with convenient Galleries,) That on the Third Monday in June next, there will be a meeting of the Vestry, at what is commonly called the Upper Church; At which Time and Place, any Person or Persons, who will undertake the same, are desired to attend, with their Plans, and Estimate of the Expence, and to give Bond, with good Security, to the Church wardens of the said Parish, for his or their true performance.
George W. Fairfax }
George Washington } Church wardens."
There is no record of a meeting of the Vestry on the third Monday in June, as specified above, and it is probable that this effort to secure a builder to undertake the Church was not successful. The present Falls Church was built a few years later by James Wren.

THE HISTORY OF TRURO PARISH

Book, and were but imperfectly known to Dr. Slaughter. He was not acquainted with the final Act of Assembly dividing the Parishes, nor had he ever seen the original and complete paper by Gen. Washington giving the result of the various elections of Vestrymen held at this time, which explains, and explains away, the seeming fact that Washington was chosen, contrary to all precedent, if not law, to serve simultaneously on the Vestries of two distinct Parishes. For these reasons Dr. Slaughter's History is, of necessity, at this point, radically imperfect; and the Editor feels that he will but carry out what would be the Author's wish, if it could be expressed, in departing from the manuscript for a few pages, and rewriting this portion of the Parish annals.]

As early as 1761 a petition was presented to the County Court, and ordered certified to the General Assembly, praying for a division of Truro Parish. The population of the County was increasing rapidly, there was an evident demand for more Churches and more services, while the health of the Rev. Mr. Green was failing. A division was the natural remedy. No action seems to have been taken further however until the year 1764. In the Journal of the House of Burgesses we read that on November 1st of that year "A petition from sundry inhabitants of the Parish of Truro, in the County of Fairfax praying that the said Parish be divided into two distinct Parishes, was pre-

THE HISTORY OF TRURO PARISH

sented to the House and read." It was referred to Messrs. George Johnston and John West, the two Burgesses from Fairfax, to prepare and bring in a Bill agreeable to the prayer of the petitioners. November 3rd. Mr. Johnston presented the Bill for dividing the Parish of Truro, and it was passed on the 6th and agreed to by the Council on the 26th. The Act provided that the division should take place from February 1st, 1765, the line being —"by Doeg creek from the mouth thereof to Mr. George Washington's mill, and from thence, by a straight line, to the plantation of John Munroe, and the same course continued to the line that divides the counties of Fairfax and Loudoun." All between this line and the Potomac was to be the new Parish of Fairfax. Each Parish was to elect its Vestry, at a time and place appointed by the Sheriff, before the second of the following April. (See Hening, VIII. 43.) The elections were held in Truro on March 25th and in Fairfax on March 28th.

This division was exceedingly favorable to the new Parish, but naturally it met with small favor in Truro. Not only was she shorn of much more than half her strength, but the congregation of Pohick, her one remaining Church, was divided, and Mount Vernon, with several other plantations which naturally belonged to this Church both from proximity and association, was now in Fairfax Parish. Accordingly when the House of Bur-

THE HISTORY OF TRURO PARISH

gesses, after a recess of several months, met again in May, we find, under date of May 14, 1765, that "A petition of sundry inhabitants of the Parish of Truro, praying a more, equal division of the said Parish, also several petitions in opposition thereto, were presented to the House and read." These were referred to the Committe of Propositions and Grivances, "to examine into, the allegations thereof, and report the same with their opinion to the House." Of this Committee Mr. Johnston was a member, as was also George Washington, who at that time represented the County of Frederick, where he was also a large freeholder. On the 15th the Committee reported two resolutions. First, that the petition from Truro, complaining of the inequality in the late division, and praying that a new division be made, by a line to begin at Clifton's or Johnson's ferry on the Potomac and to run from thence to the ford over Dogue run, and on by the line that was afterward adopted, was "reasonable." Second, that so much of the petition from Fairfax Parish in opposition thereto as prays that if the Parishes, be divided it be by other lines as therein set forth was "also reasonable." The first proposition was rejected, and the Committee ordered to bring in a Bill in accordance with the second resolution. The new Act was presented the same day and recommitted, reported with amendments on the 22d, passed the 23d, agreed to by the Council, and was signed by the

THE HISTORY OF TRURO PARISH

Governor on June 1st, so becoming a law on that date.

The preamble of this Act states that "Whereas it is represented to this present General Assembly that the lines and boundaries whereby the Parish of Truro, in the County of Fairfax, was divided into two distinct Parishes, pursuant to an Act passed for that purpose in the former part of this present session of Assembly, have made a very unequal division of the said Parish, by leaving nearly double the number of tithables in the new Parish of Fairfax than there are in Truro Parish, (sic) *Be it therefore enacted* &c. That the said Act be, and is hereby repealed, and declared null and void. *And be it further enacted*, That from and after the ninth day of June next the said Parish of Truro shall be divided into two distinct Parishes, in the following manner, that is to say; From the mouth of Little Hunting creek, up the same to the forks thereof; thence up the meanders of the south branch thereof, to the Gum Spring thereon; from thence by a straight line to the ford of Dogue run, where the back road from Colchester to Alexandria crosses the said run; and from thence by a straight line to the forks of Difficult." All above said lines to be Fairfax Parish, and all below to retain the name of Truro. New Vestries were to be elected in each Parish before the first of August following. Henry Lee, John Baylis, Foushee Tebbs, Allan Macrae, and William Car,

THE HISTORY OF TRURO PARISH

gentlemen, were appointed commissioners to adjust and divide the cost of the Glebe and improvements thereon, and of the Church plate, and the 50,000 pounds of tobacco levied for building Churches and not yet expended, between the two Parishes according to the number of tithables in each at the time of the first division. (See Hening VIII. 157.) A plot and description of the above line, made by the County Surveyor, June 15, 1765, is on record in the Clerk's office of Fairfax County.

It is evident that Washington himself, and his immense estate at Mount Vernon, was the principal bone of contention between the mother and daughter Parishes. The lines proposed ran, the one on the south, the other on the north, of the estate. The one finally adopted divided it, leaving far the larger part, however, with the mansion house, in Truro. That he would take an active interest in the settlement of the question was inevitable, and doubtless his direct agency is to be seen in the compromise petition which found favor with the House of Burgesses and was the basis of their legislation. The Act which was passed may well have been drawn by his own pen. In contrast with the previous Act it is unusually specific in its details, and would seem to indicate the hand of the Surveyor in its clearly described lines, and of the Church Warden in its accurate enumeration of the property and assets of the Parish.

But there is another silent witness to Washing-

THE HISTORY OF TRURO PARISH

ton's concern in this division. In the Library of Congress there is preserved, among his journals and some other manuscript papers, a single sheet of foolscap written on both sides in his most formal hand, and giving the result, first of the elections of Vestries for the two Parishes held in March, 1765, under the first Act of Assembly, and then of those held in July of the same year under the provisions of the second Act. The first page shows a large preponderance of voters in Fairfax Parish at the first elections, bearing out the assertion that the first division was very unequal. The second page, with the simple calculation at the bottom, shows the number of voters in the two Parishes at the second election to have been nearly the same; 334 in Fairfax and 313 in Truro. Later the Vestry Book records that the new division gave to Fairfax Parish 1013 tithables, leaving 962 in Truro.

This paper shows that at the first election, in March, 1765, Col. Washington was elected a Vestryman of the first Fairfax Parish, he being, for the moment, a resident therein. The life of this Parish was exactly four months, and of this Vestry-elect two months and three days, even if its members ever qualified or met for organization, of which there is no evidence. In July, Mount Vernon having, in the meantime, been restored to Truro, Col. Washington was again elected a Ves-

THE HISTORY OF TRURO PARISH

tryman of Truro Parish, and was not eligible in any other.

An accurate copy of this interesting paper, as written by Washington, will be found on the following pages, being here published in complete form, it is believed, for the first time.

HISTORY OF TRURO PARISH

COPY OF PAPER IN WASHINGTON'S HANDWRITING, NOW IN THE LIBRARY OF CONGRESS.

(First Page.)

VESTRY CHOSEN FOR TRURO PARISH 25th. MARCH 1765

with the Number of Votes to each.

Mr. Edward Payne 234
Colo. George Mason 210
Captn. Daniel Mc.Carty 181
Mr. Thos. Withers Coffer 174
Mr. William Gardner 169
Colo. George Wm. Fairfax ..161
Mr. Alexr. Henderson 158
Captn. Lewis Ellzey 152
Mr. Thomison Ellzey 151
Mr. Thomas Ford 151
Mr. John Ford 141
Majr. Peter Wagener 126

Candidates then rejected

Doctr. Cookburn
Mr. Benja. Grayson
Mr. Joshua Furguson
Mr. Edward Washington
Mr. William Baylis
Mr. Henry Boggess
Mr. William Linton
Mr. Marmaduke Beckwith
Mr. John Thompson
Mr. Thomas Lucas
Mr. George Simpson
Mr. Benja. Talbot
Mr. Joseph Bennet
Mr. John Daniel
Mr. John Monroe
Mr. James Halley

VESTRY CHOSEN FOR FAIRFAX PARISH 28th. MARCH 1765

with the Number of Votes to each

Colo. John West 340
Mr. Charles Alexander 309
Mr. William Payne 304
Captn. John Dalton 281
C. Geo. Washington 274
Majr. Chs. Broadwater 260
Captn. George Johnston 254
Mr. Townsend Dade 252
Mr. Richd. Sanford 247
Mr. Willm. Adams 244
Captn. Posey 222
Mr. Daniel French 221

Candidates then rejected

Mr. Thomas Wren 220
Mr. James Wren 205
Mr. Edward Blackburn 204
Mr. John West Junr. 199
Mr. Edward Dulan 199
Mr. Benja. Sebastian 160
Mr. James Donaldson 131
Mr. Henry Gunnel 126
Mr. John Seal 120
Mr. Charles Thrift 112
Captn. Sampson Darrell ....

HISTORY OF TRURO PARISH

(Second Page.)

VESTRY CHOSEN FOR TRURO PARISH 22d. JULY 1765 with the Number of Votes for each.	VESTRY CHOSEN FOR FAIRFAX PARISH 25th. JULY 1765 with the Number of Votes for each.
Colo. Geo. Mason 282	Colo. West 309
Captn. Edwd. Payne 277	Mr. William Payne 289
Colo. Geo. Washington 259	Mr. William Adams 250
Captn. John Posey 259	Captn. John Dalton 247
Captn. Daniel Mc.Carty 246	Mr. Thos. Wren 237
Colo. Geo. Wm. Fairfax......235	Mr. Edward Dulan 228
Mr. Alexander Henderson ..231	Majr. Chs. Broadwater 225
Mr. William Gardner 218	Mr. Richard Sanford........225
Mr. Thomison Ellzey 209	Mr. Daniel French 216
Mr. Thos. Withers Coffer 189	Mr. Edward Blackburn......210
Mr. Wiliam Lynton 173	Mr. Thos. Shaw 209
Mr. Thomas Ford 170	Mr. Townsend Dade 205
Mr. Henry Boggess 168	Mr. James Wren 205
Mr. Joshua Furguson 162	Mr. Charles Alexander 204
Mr. Edward Washington 154	Mr. Robert Alexander 204
Mr. George Simpson 153	Captn. George Johnston 183
Majr. Peter Wagener 146	Mr. Sampson Darrel 151
Mr. Benja. Grayson 139	Mr. Benja. Sebastian 150
Mr. William Baylis 86	Mr. Presley Cox 85
Whole Number of Votes....3756	Whole Number of Votes....4012

12/3756/313 Number of Voters

15

36

..

12/4012/334 Number of Voters

41

52

4

THE HISTORY OF TRURO PARISH

Jared Sparks, in his Life of Washington and also in the Writings of Washington which he edited, not understanding the meaning of this paper nor Washington's obvious purpose in preparing it, published a small part of it only, namely the two lists of Vestrymen elected, the one in Fairfax Parish on March 28th and the other in Truro Parish on July 22d, in which the name of Washington appears. He thus gave rise to the groundless tradition, which has been so generally adopted and perpetuated by succeeding writers, that Washington *served as a Vestryman* in both of these Parishes, and presumably at the same time, though Sparks is careful not to assert this. But had he published the whole paper the error would not have arisen.

Bishop Meade says he had seen a printed list of these Vestries which was supposed to have come from "A leaf of the old Pohick Vestry Book which had by some means gotten into the Historical Society of New York." Dr. Slaughter, at this place, gives this list as "Verified by Mrs. Burton Harrison, who kindly inspected the missing leaf in the New York Historical Society rooms and sent me a copy of it." This list agrees substantially with that given by Sparks, as do they both, *as far as they go,* with the original list written by Washington, though both omit the titles before the different names which Washington, with old-fashioned punctiliousness, was so careful to give. The New

THE HISTORY OF TRURO PARISH

York list, however, whatever its source, is not from a leaf of the Vestry Book as Bishop Meade understood.

One frequently finds the assertion made by careless writers that Washington was a Vestryman of Pohick, or some other, *Church*. Such a statement is, of course, inaccurate, and Washington himself would hardly have understood what was meant by it. In his day Vestries in Virginia were confined to Parishes, usually containing two or three Churches. Pohick is the only Church remaining which stood in Washington's time in the Parish of which he was a Vestryman. The present Falls Church and Christ Church, Alexandria, were built in Fairfax Parish soon after its separation from Truro.

The Vestry chosen for Truro at the *March* elections held but one meeting. This was on April 26, 1765, at the house of Samuel Littlejohn.

[We now resume the thread of the History as written by Dr. Slaughter.]

During the current year the Minister of the Parish, the Rev. Charles Green, departed this life. There is no formal notice of his decease in the Vestry Book. It was not the custom of the times to pass resolutions on such occasions. It is only referred to in the business items, four months' salary due being ordered paid to his executor. Falls Church and Alexandria were no longer in Truro, so it became possible to have another place of worship. Accordingly the Vestry rented from Samuel Littlejohn the tobacco house on his plantation for one thousand pounds of tobacco a year, until a Church could be built in the upper part of the present Parish, he agreeing to keep it clean and provide water for the congregation. An agreement was made with John Robertson to fit up this house with six benches the length of the house and two at the ends; a reading desk and Communion table, with a small window on each side of the desk; to lay plank on the joists the width of eight feet, with a rail in front, and two broad step ladders, and to stop the eaves; all to be done in the plainest manner, within six months, for 1400 pounds of tobacco. When the house was given up the plank used was to remain for the use of the Parish.

The Rev. James Scott, of Dettingen Parish, the grandfather of the late Judge Scott, of Fauquier, often officiated in Truro in the interval between the Rev. Mr. Green and his successor, Mr. Massey. He received payment altogether for forty sermons, at 332 pounds of tobacco each. The Rev. John Andrews, of Cameron Parish, also preached twice, at the same rate.

The Vestry, (that elected in July,) had a protracted meeting on the 28th, 29th and 30th of November, 1765, when the accounts between the two Parishes were settled as far as could be done at

THE HISTORY OF TRURO PARISH

that time. The settlement is spread upon the minutes in full, but is uninteresting.*

It was ordered, That the agreement made with Samuel Littlejohn by the former Vestry be continued; That Elijah Williams be appointed Reader at Littlejohn's, and that he attend there to read Divine Service every Sunday, and that he be paid at the rate of 1000 pounds of tobacco a year; That Mr. George Johnston be appointed to act as Attorney for the Parish, and that he return a list of all the judgments obtained by him to the Church Wardens by the first of November annually; and That the Vestry meet at Mr. William Gardner's on first Monday in February next to agree with workmen to undertake the building of a brick Church to contain 1600 superficial feet; the Church Wardens to advertise the same in as public a manner as may be, and each workman to bring a plan and estimate of expense. George Mason and Edward Payne were continued as Church Wardens for the next year, and the latter was appointed Collector of the Parish Levy, giving bond and security as was the custom.† John Barry was con-

---

*An echo of the contest over the Parish lines is found in two items charged against Truro: "To Mr. Thomizen Ellzey for running the line from Johnson's ferry to the fork of Difficult," and "To Majr. Wagener for copying six lists of tithables in April, 1765."

†The Levy this year was 60 pounds of tobacco per poll, as against from 20 to 37 pounds for many years before the division. It continued to range at from 60 to 80 pounds for six years following, while Payne's and the new Pohick Churches were being built, after which it gradually fell to about the former average. It is probable that the Vestrymen themselves paid one-half of the tithes of the Parish, Washington and Mason being doubtless the largest ratepayers.

49

THE HISTORY OF TRURO PARISH

tinued as Clerk of the Vestry; and the third Friday in November annually was appointed as a day for meeting.

Payne's Church

"At a Vestry held for Truro Parish at William Gardner's on the 3rd and 4th days of February, 1766—
    Present, Mr. Edwd. Payne, C. W.
Colo. Geo. Washington   Mr. William Gardner
Capt. Daniel Mc.Carty   Thomas Withers Coffer
Colo. Geo. Wm. Fairfax   Wm. Linton &
Mr. Alexr. Henderson   Thos. Ford
                                    Vestrymen.

Who being there met to enquire the most convenient place to erect a new Church, and to agree with workmen to build the same.

"Resolved, that the new Church be built on the middle Ridge near the Ox road, the ground to be laid off by Mr. Edward Payne, Mr. William Gardner, Mr. Thos. Withers Coffer and Mr. Thos. Ford, or any three of them, on the land supposed to be belonging to Mr. Thomazen Ellzey, who being present consents to the same.

"Agreeable to a plan and articles annexed thereto Mr. Edward Payne hath undertaken to build the said Church for the sum of five hundred and seventy-nine pounds Virginia Currency.

"Ordered that the said Edward Payne do paint

Payne's Church, 1768-1862. From a Photograph taken in 1861

THE HISTORY OF TRURO PARISH

the cornish, windows and doors of the said Church and bring in his charge thereof. And that he pay to Mr. John Ayres forty shillings for his plan and estimate.

"Ordered that Col. Geo. Washington, Capt. Daniel McCarty, Colo. Geo. Wm. Fairfax, Mr. Alex. Henderson and Mr. Thos. Ford, or any three of them, do view and examine the said building from time to time as shall be requisite.

"Ordered that 31,549 lb. of tobo. in the hands of the Church Wardens for the year 1764, to wit, George Washington and George Wm. Fairfax Esqrs. be sold to the highest bidder, before the Court House door of this County on the first day of June Court next between the hours of 12 and 4, and that publick notice be given of the sale."

"MEMORANDUM of an Agreement made this fourth day of February one thousand seven hundred and sixty six, between the Vestry of Truro Parish in the County of Fairfax and Edward Payne of the Parish of Truro and County aforesaid as follows, vizt.—

"The said Edward Payne does undertake and agree to build and finish in a Workman like manner a Church on the Ox Road, to be placed agreeable to an order of the said Vestry, of the following Demensions & according to the annexed Plan, to wit, Fifty three and an half feet in length, and thirty feet in breadth in the Clear; the walls to be built of good Bricks, well burnt, of the ordinary size, that is nine Inches long, four and an half Inches broad, and three Inches thick, the outside Bricks to be laid with Mortar two thirds lime and one third sand, the inside Bricks to be laid with Mortar half lime and half sand. The Corners of the House, the Windows & Doors, to be of rubb'd Brick—The Arches and Pediment heads of the Doors and Windows to be of Bricks rubbed gauged and set in Putty.

"The Doors to be made of Pine Plank, two Inches thick, moulded and raised Pannells on both sides.

"The Sashes to be made of Pine Plank, one Inch and three quarters thick, and to have Sixteen lights in each square Sash, of the best crown-Glass, twelve Inches by ten. The Window and Door Cases to be made with double Archatraves.

"The floors and Gallery to be framed with good Oak, the Roof to be framed with good Poplar—and the Scantling to be of a size and proper Proportion to the Building.

"The Roof to be covered with Inch pine Plank cyphered and lapt, one and an half Inches. And to be Shingled with good Cypress Shingles, twenty Inches in length and to show six Inches.

"The Cornish to be in Proportion to the hight of the Walls (which are to be twenty two feet and an half,) with Dentile Blocks.

"The floors to be laid with pine Plank, one and an half Inch thick, the Iles to be laid with Brick

THE HISTORY OF TRURO PARISH

Tyles, the Pews to be wainscotted with Pine plank, an Inch and an half thick, double work on each side of the framing and raised pannel on one side.

"To have an Altar Piece sixteen feet high & twelve feet wide, and done with wainscot after the Ionic order. The floor of the Communion place to be raised twelve Inches higher than the floor of the house with hand rails and Banisters of black Walnut.

"The Pulpit, Canopy and reading Desks to be of black walnut, Wainscoted with proper Cornish.

"The Gallery to be supported by Collums turned & fluted, to come out as far as the second Window at the West end of the Church, to have a Wainscoted front, and to have four Seats raised one behind and above another. The whole to be done and finished by the first Day of October in the Year one thousand seven hundred and Sixty eight, in sufficient and workmanlike manner, agreeable to the Plan aforesaid.

"In Consideration whereof the said Vestry do agree to pay unto the said Edward Payne the sum of Five hundred and Seventy nine pounds Virginia Currency in manner following to wit, one third part of the said sum to be paid on the first Day of July next—another third part when the Church is covered, and the remaining part when the whole work is compleated and finished. In Witness whereof the said Parties (to wit) the Members of the said Vestry here Present and the said Edward

THE HISTORY OF TRURO PARISH

Payne have hereunto interchangeably set their Hands the Day and Year first above written.

"The said Edward Payne is also to Ceil, Plaister & Whitewash the inside of the said Church in a proper manner, and to find and put on Locks and Hinges on the Doors & hinges on the Pews &c.

"Signed &c.   Go. Washington
in presence of   Daniel Mc.Carty
Lee Massey   Go. Wm. Fairfax
John Barry   A. Henderson
John Tillett   William Gardner
                       Thos. Withers Coffer
                       William Linton
                       Thos. Ford
A true copy   Edwd. Payne.
Test, John Barry, Clk. Vestry."

THE REV. LEE MASSEY, SECOND RECTOR

At this same meeting of the Vestry the following action was taken: "Whereas Mr. Lee Massey, an Inhabitant of this Parish, having this day offered to supply the place of a Minister therein, and the Vestry being of opinion that he is a person well qualified for the sacred function, have agreed to recommend him to the favour of His Grace the Bishop of London and of the Governor of this Colony, for an Introduction to this said Parish, and to receive him upon his return properly qualified to discharge the said office."

THE HISTORY OF TRURO PARISH

"In consequence of the aforesaid Resolve a Recommendation to his Lordship the Bishop of London, and an address to his Honour the Governor of this Colony in favour of Mr. Lee Massey being made out, are ordered hereafter to be recorded."

"At a Vestry held for Truro Parish in the County of Fairfax and Colony of Virginia, the fourth day of February in the year of our Lord one thousand seven hundred and sixty six.
To His Grace the Bishop of London.

Whereas Mr. Lee Massey purposes to enter into holy Orders and hath applied to this Vestry for their Recommendation to his Grace the Bishop of London and to his Honour the Governor of Virginia and offers and engages so soon as he shall be properly Ordained to return to Virginia and receive and accept of this Parish of Truro now vacant by the death of the late Rector, the Reverend Mr. Charles Green, Provided we will keep the same vacant for him during our right of Patronage, or the Governor will be pleased to induct him into it, if the Vestry's right of Patronage is expired when he returns. And the said Lee Massey having lived several years amongst us and his moral Character and unexceptionable Life and Conversation being well known to most of us, we beg leave to recommend him to his Grace the Bishop of London as a Person well qualified for the Sacred Function, and also to the Favor of the

THE HISTORY OF TRURO PARISH

Honourable Francis Fauquier Esqr. Governor of this Colony, and humbly entreat him to induct the said Mr. Lee Massey into this Parish of Truro in case he should return after the expiration of our right of Patronage, On which condition we do hereby agree and oblige ourselves to keep the said Parish vacant accordingly, and to receive and provide for the said Mr. Lee Massey as Rector thereof according to the Laws of this Colony.

In Testimony whereof we being Vestrymen of the said Parish of Truro, (and all that are now present,) have hereunto set our hands the day and year above written.

Edwd. Payne	Go. Washington
Daniel Mc.Carty	Go. Wm. Fairfax
A. Henderson	William Gardner
Thos. Withers Coffer	Thos. Ford
	William Linton

Copy. John Barry, Clk. Vestry.

Fairfax County, Truro Parish, Feby. 4th, 1766.
Sir,

We the Vestry of Truro Parish beg leave to recommend to yr. Honour's Notice and Favour, the Bearer, Mr. Lee Massey, who has an Intention of entering into holy Orders, provided he can have a certainty of this Parish, and as his Character and Personal Merit is well known to us, we are very desirous of receiving him, and have given him the best Title in our Power. But it being

THE HISTORY OF TRURO PARISH

probable that he cannot return from England while the Parish remains in our disposal, we most earnestly recommend him to your Honour's good offices herein, and if you will be pleased to favour him with an Induction or Presentation to this Parish, in case he returns after the Expiration of our right, we will engage to keep the same vacant for him as long as it is in our power.* An answer will very particularly oblige,—Your Honour's most obedt. humble Servants.—

Edwd. Payne	Go. Washington
Daniel Mc.Carty	Go. Wm. Fairfax
A. Henderson	William Gardner
Thos. Withers Coffer	Thos. Ford
	William Linton

To the Hon.ble Francis Fauquier Esqr. Lieut. Governor of Virginia.

Copy.

Test John Barry Clk. Vestry.

At a Vestry held July 10th, 1766, there were present as above with the addition of Col. George

---

*These letters recall the old contest between the Governors and the Vestries in regard to the right of presentation and the induction of Ministers into the Parishes. The early Governors claimed the right of Patronage as the representatives of the Crown, and in some instances sought to exercise it by forcing unwelcome Ministers upon certain Parishes. But the claim, or at least its enforcement, was vigorously resisted. Many of the Vestries adopted the plan of electing their Ministers year by year, thus avoiding a vacancy but saving the risk of having an inefficient or unworthy Minister saddled upon them and drawing his legal salary for life. A law passed in 1748 declared the sole right of presentation to remain in the Vestry for twelve months after a vacancy occurred. After that it was supposed to rest with the Governor. This is the law the Vestry here had in mind. Fortunately the Vestry of Truro was saved from all trouble in respect to their Ministers by being able to choose good men already known to them and sending them to England for orders.

THE HISTORY OF TRURO PARISH

Mason. Church Warden Edward Payne, who had been previously directed to enquire into certain deficiencies in the work ordered done on the Falls Church in 1763, reported that he had applied to the persons formerly appointed to view this work and they had denied having had any orders to view the same and refused to concern themselves. Whereupon it was ordered that Thomas Price view the work and report what deficiencies appear therein, that Mr. Payne attend as representative of this Vestry and request the Fairfax Vestry to appoint a workman and one of their members to attend the view on behalf of their Parish. Tobacco on hand was ordered to be sold at July and August Courts.

At the regular meeting in November the Parish Levy was laid, amounting to 55,860 pounds of tobacco; of which 35,000 was for "building Churches." Col. George Washington and Mr. William Gardner were appointed Church Wardens for the ensuing year, and were ordered to receive the money due from George Washington, Geo. Wm. Fairfax, Capt. McCarty and William Payne, former Church Wardens, and pay Edward Payne what was due to him. Mr. Gardner was also appointed Collector.

1767. February 23d. At a Vestry held this day there were present George Washington Esqr. and Mr. William Gardner, Church Wardens, and Messrs. Mason, Payne, Posey, McCarty, Hender-

THE HISTORY OF TRURO PARISH

son, Coffer, Linton, and Thomazen Ellzey. "Pursuant to an Act of the General Assembly entitled an Act to empower the Vestry of Truro Parish in the County of Fairfax to sell their Glebe and Church Plate—Ordered that the said Glebe and Church Plate be sold at Public Vendue on Friday the 22d of May next. The sale to be upon the premises, and the Purchaser or Purchasers to be allowed eighteen months credit, giving bond with good security."

The Church Wardens were ordered to employ a Surveyor to run the lines of the Glebe land and to make a plot thereof. Also to advertise the same with a proper description of land and improvements, and the Church plate, in the Virginia and Maryland Gazettes.

"The Rev. Lee Massey having produced to this Vestry a presentation to the Rectory, Benefice and Cure of this Parish under the hand of Francis Fauquier Esqr. Lieutenant Governor &c. of Virginia and under the Seal of the Colony, dated January the 14th. 1767, Ordered that the said Lee Massey be accordingly received into this Parish as Minister thereof, and be provided for pursuant to the Laws of this Colony." Mr. Massey was also allowed "the Annual Sum of 4000 pounds of tobacco in lieu of a Glebe until one is purchased."

James Wren and Thomas Price, the workmen appointed to view the work done to Falls Church, reported that there appeared to be a deficiency

THE HISTORY OF TRURO PARISH

in the work of nine pounds fourteen shillings and sixpence. The Church Wardens were ordered to "apply to Maj. Charles Broadwater (the Undertaker of the said work) for the said sum and account with the Vestry of Fairfax Parish for their proportion of the same when it is received."

"Ordered that a Vestry House be built at the new Church of the dimensions and in manner following Vizt. of Brick, twenty by sixteen feet, with a large inside chimney, nine feet pitch from the Foundation, with Brick or Tile floor, covered with Cypress Shingles, Ceiling and Walls Plaistered and whitewashed, one pannell Door in the broad side, with a Sash Window with twelve Lights and pannel Shutters opposite. Barge board and Cornis. The Barge boards and Cornis, Door Window and Shutters to be painted, a **Lock** to the Door. The said House to be furnished with a Table and three Benches, for making which and the Cornis the Undertaker to be allowed a sufficiency of Planks out of the Parishes Plank now in Samuel Littlejohn's Tobacco House." All was to be finished by Christmas, and Edward Payne undertook the work for Fifty one pounds ten shillings, current money.

The Vestry met again on May 22d., the day of the sale, at the Glebe. Present, Rev. Lee Massey, Minister, George Washington and William Gardner Church Wardens, and Messrs. Mason, Payne, Mc.Carty, Posey and Linton.

THE HISTORY OF TRURO PARISH

"Mr. Thomazen Ellzey having returned a Plott of a Survey made of the Glebe Land, pursuant to a former order of the Vestry, containing three hundred eighty five Acres and an half only, which said Quantity of Land being exposed to sale to the highest Bidder was purchased by Daniel Mc.Carty Gent. at the price of Three hundred and twenty two pounds Virginia Currency, who gave his Bond with Mr. Richard Chichester his Security for the same, payable eighteen months hence, to George Washington and William Gardner, Church Wardens, for the Use of this Parish."

"The Church Plate being also exposed to sale, was purchased by the said Daniel Mc.Carty, at the price of Twenty six pounds, Virginia Currency, for the Use of the Parish."

The Vestry met again July 25th, 1767. Present, Col. Washington and Mr. Gardner, Church Wardens, and Messrs. Payne, Mc.Carty, Fairfax, Henderson, Ellzey and Linton. George Washington and George William Fairfax exhibited accounts of tobacco levied in 1763, and the sale thereof and payments made to Edward Payne. Account received and approved. Mr. Payne exhibited similar accounts of tobacco levied in 1765, and of money received by him for building the new Church and the balance still due, which were approved. Tobacco in the hands of William Gardner, Collector, ordered sold. Balance due Mr. Payne on second payment for the Church to be

THE HISTORY OF TRURO PARISH

paid, and the residue of the money to remain in the Collector's hands, he giving bond with fresh security for its payment when demanded.

Col. George Mason, Capt. McCarty, Mr. Ellzey and Mr. Linton appointed to view the new Vestry House, and if they receive the same the Collector to pay Mr. Payne the contract price.

"George William Fairfax Esqr. having consented to import for the Use of this Parish (at the Risque of the Parish) two folio Prayer Books and a Quarto Bible, Ordered that upon receipt thereof the Church Wardens for the time being pay him for the same, if they have so much money in their hands."

Orders for Processioning:—James Halley Sen, and Moses Simpson, between Occoquan, the Ox road and the County line. George Simpson and William Keen, between the Ox road and the Backlick road from the Parish line down to the road that leads from Cameron by the Glebe to where it crosses Pohic, below Robert Boggess'. William Triplett and Joseph Cash, between the Backlick road, the Parish line, Potowmack river and Pohic Creek.

On September 28th, 1767, the Vestry met for the fifth time during this fiscal year. Present, Rev. Lee Massey, Washington, Gardner, Mason, Posey, Payne, Coffer, Ellzey and Ford. The minutes recite several former orders for the sale of tobacco and payments to be made by the Col-

THE HISTORY OF TRURO PARISH

lector, none of which had been complied with except one sale of 15,000 pounds to Mr. Hector Ross, for which his note was now given to the Church Wardens; it was ordered that Mr. Ross pay Mr. Payne what was due him on the second payment for the Church and for the Vestry House when it should be received by the viewers. And the Collector was to account with the Vestry at its next meeting for the tobacco remaining in his hands.

The New Pohick Church

1767. The annual meeting for laying the Parish Levy was held November 20th. Present, the entire Vestry.

"Resolved, that a Church be built at or as near the Cross Road leading from Hollis's to Pohic Warehouse as water can be had, which resolution was carried by a majority of seven to five."

Bishop Meade has handed down a tradition as to the part which Washington took in the location of this Church. Although no allusion is made to it in the Vestry Book it is good enough to be true and therefore we reproduce it, as follows: "The Old Pohick Church was a frame building, and occupied a site on the south side of Pohick run, and about two miles from the present site which is on the north side of the run. When it was no longer fit for use, it is said the parishioners

THE HISTORY OF TRURO PARISH

were called together to determine on the locality of the new Church, when George Mason, the compatriot of Washington, advocated the old site, pleading that it was the house in which their fathers worshipped, and that the graves of many were around it, while Washington and others advocated a more central and convenient one. The question was left unsettled, and another meeting for its decision appointed. Meanwhile Washington surveyed the neighborhood, and marked the houses and distances on a well-drawn map, and, when the day of decision arrived, met all the arguments of his opponent by presenting this paper, and thus carried his point." It was the Vestry, however, and not the parishioners, who fixed on the site. The old site was nearer to Gunston and the new one nearer Mount Vernon.*

To return to this Vestry meeting:—It was "Ordered, that Mr. William Grayson be appointed Attorney for this Parish, and that he be paid fees only upon such suits as he obtains judgments for."

The Collector being still not ready to settle his accounts a special Vestry was appointed to meet in March following to receive from him the to-

---

*This story is given by Sparks in his Life of Washington, and is repeated by Lossing and others. The first discussion probably took place at the Vestry held on September 28th, at which time both Mason and Washington were present but four Vestrymen were absent. The question would naturally be deferred until Messrs. Fairfax, Henderson, Mc.Carty and Linton could be heard, and no mention of a fruitless debate would be made on the minutes. The interest taken in the matter, and perhaps the opposition to the new site, is indicated by the full attendance at this Vestry, and by the mention made of the vote by which the change in location was adopted.

THE HISTORY OF TRURO PARISH

bacco due, and the Clerk was ordered to give his securities notice thereof.

The Parish accounts, to meet which the annual Levy was laid, are given in full for this year, Washington having been Church Warden and principal administrator of Parish affairs.

	Tobacco.	Dr. £.	s.	d.
To Rev. Lee Massey's salary..	17,280			
John Barry, Clk. of Pohic....	1,000			
Elijah Williams, do. Littlejohn's	1,000			
Do. for three days extra attendance	60			
Mr. Peter Wagener, Clerk of the County	627			
Rev. Lee Massey, in lieu of a Glebe	4,000			
Rev. James Scott, for 6 sermons	1,992			
Samuel Littlejohn, Sexton, &c...	1,000			
Charles Wright, Do. at Pohic	560			
Grafton Kirk for maintg. Sarah Jackson	400			
William Cullison, per acct....		1	0	0
John Hollis, for the board of Dorothy Chesher, from the 25th. of May to this date..	200			

THE HISTORY OF TRURO PARISH

Samuel Russell for his support, he being allowed to remove to Cameron Parish, his claim to continue......	500		
Mr. William Grayson, per acct		6	0	0
Doctr. James Nisbett, per acct.		8	15	0
George Washington Esqr. per acct.		1	13	9
George Mason Esqr. for finding ellaments twice........	200		
William Gardner, bal. per acct. as Church Warden, exclusive of the Collection acct. that not being settled......	500 &	3	12	3
Robert Loyd, for his support..	500		
John Hollis, for his support..	500		
(These were also exempted from paying Levy in future.)			
Thomazen Ellzey, per acct..		3	10	8
John Barry, Clk. Vestry, salary and extra services....	850		
Charles Wright, for making a back and hearth..........			5	0
Thomazen Ellzey, for extra services		5	0	0
Tobacco for building a Church	7,000		
	38,169	29	16	0

THE HISTORY OF TRURO PARISH

To 6 per Ct. for Collecting
38,169 lb. of Tobo........ 2,290
To a fraction in the Collectors
hands 254

                               40,713
               Cr.
By 993 Tithables at 41 lbs. of
Tobacco per Poll.........40,713

Cash accounts due ordered paid out of money in hands of Mr. Hector Ross. John Posey and Thomazen Ellzey appointed Church Wardens for the next year.

1768. March 5th. Mr. Gardner settled his account by paying 18,011 lbs. of transfer tobacco and 25 pounds in cash, which were lodged in the hands of George Mason Esqr. Mr. Gardner to have the privilege of exchanging four hogsheads of his own crop for transfer tobacco, and to redeem the money with 2,101 lbs. of transfer tobacco.

"Ordered, that Hector Ross pay out of the money in his hands to George William Fairfax Esqr. the sum of sixteen pounds, seventeen shillings current money, agreeable to the account lodged for surplices and books imported by him for the use of the Parish."

At a Vestry held at the new Church, (Payne's,) September 9th, 1768,* to view and examine the

---
*From Washington's diary, 1768. "Septr. 9. Proceeded (from Alexandria) to the meeting of our Vestry at the new Church and

THE HISTORY OF TRURO PARISH

work, they found it to be completed according to agreement except the brick pediments over the doors, "And being of opinion that the house can receive no damage from the weather for want of the pediments, and understanding that it is the general desire of the people in this part of the Parish to have the Church received, on account of the great inconvenience they at present suffer for want of it, we do accordingly receive the said Church for the use of the Parish, except the pediments, which the said Edward Payne is still liable for and obliged to finish according to the Articles of Agreement." Col. George Mason was ordered to make to Mr. Payne the last payment on the Church, and also to pay an account for "making horse-blocks and benches, clearing the Churchyard, and for some additional work done to the Church over and above his agreement, which we think of service and ornament to the building." Messrs. Ford, Linton and Ellzey "dissented to receiving the Church."*

---

lodgd at Captn. Edwd. Paynes." This Church was about seventeen miles from Alexandria.

On July 16, 1768, he "Went by Muddy Hole and Doeg Run to the Vestry at Pohick Church stayed there till half after 3 oclock & only 4 members coming returned by Captn. Mc.Cartys and dined there."

*This Church is hereafter known in the Vestry Book as the Upper Church, but probably from the beginning was popularly known as Payne's Church. It stood on the present road from Fairfax Court House to Fairfax Station, two and a half miles from the former and one mile from the latter. Its fate was that of many of its contemporaries. After the Revolution it was disused except for perhaps occasional services. Early in the last century the Baptists took possession of it as abandoned property, as the judgments of the Courts allowed them to do, and upon the division in that denomination in 1840 the Jerusalem Baptist Church, (New School,) was organized in the building and continued to use it until 1862.

THE HISTORY OF TRURO PARISH

November 28, 1768,—The Levy includes 15,000 lbs. of tobacco for building a Church. Daniel Mc.Carty Gent. and Thos. Withers Coffer appointed Church Wardens. Alex. Henderson and George Mason exhibited accounts of moneys from sales of tobacco which were approved. George Washington was ordered to pay Mr. Henderson eight Pounds, being balance in his hands of the sum received from Major Broadwater for deficiency in work done on the Falls Church. Mr. Henderson was also to receive from Capt. Mc.Carty 372 Pounds due on the purchase of the Glebe. William Weston's offer to cover the Vestry House at Pohick, the Vestry finding the nails, and to keep it always clean and in good order for the purposes of the Vestry, for permission to make use of the said house, was accepted. Edward Payne was authorized to open a window in the west end of the upper Church to give light and air to the gallery, and bring in his account. It was Ordered that the Church to be built be of brick, and contain three thousand square feet from outside to outside; and that the Church Wardens

---

Other Denominations also held occasional services there. The building remained unaltered, and many of our old citizens remember its ancient interior. In the winter of 1862-63 a large body of Federal troops were encamped in the vicinity, and by them the fine old Church was torn down, brick by brick, and the material used to build chimneys and hearths for their winter quarters. The tombstones in the large graveyard perhaps shared the same fate, for only one or two remain, though the yard is full of sunken graves. A small frame Baptist Church now covers part of the site of old Payne's, the foundation lines of which can still be traced.

The silver Communion service belonging to this Church was given by an old lady living in the neighborhood to the Rev. W. F. Lockwood about the year 1850, and was by him presented to St. John's Church, Centerville, where it is still in use.

THE HISTORY OF TRURO PARISH

give notice in the Virginia and Maryland Gazettes for workmen to attend at Pohick on the first Friday in March with plans and estimates.

At a Vestry held March 3d. 1769,
Present, the Rev. Lee Massey, Minister,
Daniel Mc.Carty,
Thos. Withers Coffer,
Church Wardens,

George Wm. Fairfax   Edwd. Payne
George Washington   Thomazen Ellzey
George Mason   Wm. Gardner
           Esqrs.   Wm. Linton
Alex. Henderson   Thos. Ford
                        Vestrymen.

"The Vestry having met pursuant to a former order to let the building of the new Church at Pohic,—Mr. Daniel French undertook the building the new Church at the Cross Roads, for the sum of £877 Virginia Currency."

"Ordered, that Mr. Alexander Henderson pay to Mr. James Wren and Mr. William Wait each forty shillings, out of the money in his hands, for the plans furnished the Vestry."* Adjourned,

---

*This would seem at first glance to dispose of the tradition that Washington drew the plans for the present Pohick Church. Lossing states, however, that he had before him, when he wrote, the original plan and elevation which Washington drew, and gives a cut of them. But he does not say how he knew them to have been the original plans. Washington was very apt to possess himself of a copy of such papers. The true story is possibly this: that the plans and specifications adopted were a composite of those

THE HISTORY OF TRURO PARISH

"not having completed their business," until April 7th. (But no meeting was held on that date.)

"At a Vestry held for Truro Parish at the Cross Roads leading from Hollis's to Pohick Warehouse Sepr. 21st. 1769.—

"A spott was chosen to fix the new Church upon convenient to the said Cross Roads, and agreeable to a former order of the Vestry, bearing date the 20th. day of November, 1767. A yard was laid off for the said Church, and a certain quantity of land laid off for the use of the said Parish, for which the said Vestry do agree to pay Daniel French Gent. at the rate of one Guinea per acre, for what the same shall measure.

"At the same time the said Daniel French, who on the third day of March last undertook to build the Church for the sum of eight hundred seventy and seven Pounds, Current Money of Virginia, agreeable to a plan then exhibited, did execute an

---

presented by Mr. Wren, Mr. Wait(e) and perhaps Mr. French who received the contract, and were practically drawn up in detail at this prolonged meeting of the Vestry. In this work Washington would doubtless have a large share. In his journal he mentions this meeting: "Mar. 3d. Went to a Vestry at Pohick Church and returned abt. 11 o'clock at night." The Vestry Book says they adjourned to April 7th, "Not having completed their business," that is not having drawn and signed the contract. As the Vestry usually met early in the afternoon they had probably given six or seven hours to the work, which would indicate very careful consideration and perhaps some differences of opinion to be reconciled.

The same general plan was followed in building all four of the Churches erected in Fairfax and Alexandria at about this time. It was quite the usual one of the period, omitting for the sake of economy the tower and the cruciform shape common in the Churches of an earlier date. The tower of Christ Church, Alexandria, is of comparatively recent construction, being less than a century old. The Falls Church was built by Mr. James Wren, and may represent the plan which he submitted to this Vestry.

71

THE HISTORY OF TRURO PARISH

agreement and gave bond for the performance thereof, agreeable to a contract entered into with the Vestry on the said third day of March, and ordered to be ratified and confirmed, by certain instruments in writing on the seventh day of April following, but which for want of a meeting of the Vestry on that day, and the frequent disappointments since, has never been done till now."†

"Resolved, that the Church Wardens procure from the said Daniel French a proper conveyance of the lot or parcell of land aforementioned." They were also directed to receive from Mr. Henderson the money in his hands due the Parish and pay Mr. French 200 Pounds, the first payment for the new Church.

A Notable Building Committee

"Resolved, that the Honble. George Wm. Fairfax, George Washington & George Mason Esqrs. Captn. Daniel Mc.Carty & Mr. Edward Payne do view and examine the building from time to time, as they or any three of them shall see fitting, to

---

†Washington's diary casts some light on these "frequent disappointments," and would seem to indicate that they were not wholly accidental.
(1769) "Apl. 7. Went a fox hunting in the morning and catchd a dog fox after running him an hour and treeing twice. After this went to an intended meeting of ye Vestry but there was none."
"July 24. Went to an intended Vestry at ye Cross Roads, but was disappointed of one by Mr. Hendersons refusing to act." Mr. Henderson, living at Colchester, was probably one of the Vestrymen who joined with Col. Mason in opposing the new site for the Church. Is it possible that the art of filibustering was not unknown in those days?

THE HISTORY OF TRURO PARISH

whom the undertaker is to give notice when the different materials are ready."

"ARTICLES OF AGREEMENT made the seventh day of April in the year 1769. Between the Vestry of Truro Parish in County of Fairfax, of the one part, and Daniel French of Fairfax Parish in the County aforesaid, Gent. of the other part, as follows, Vizt. The said Daniel French doth undertake and agree to build and finish in a workmanlike manner a Church, near the forks of the roads above Robert Boggess's, to be placed as the Vestry shall hereafter direct, of the following Dimensions and Materials, to Wit; Sixty six feet in length, and forty five feet and a half in breadth, from out to out, the Walls twenty eight feet high from the foundation, to be built of good bricks well burnt, of the ordinary size, that is, nine inches long, four and a half inches broad, and three inches thick, to be three bricks thick to the Water Table, and two and a half afterwards. The outside bricks to be laid with mortar two thirds lime and one of sand, and the inside with mortar half lime and half sand. The corners of the House, the Pedistals, and Doors with the Pediment heads to be of good white freestone, and the Returns and Arches of the Windows to be of rubbed brick. The Doors to be made of pine plank, two inches thick, moulded and raised pannells on both sides, and the frames thereof to be of pine clear of sap, with locust sills. The Window frames to be of pine clear of sap, with locust sills; the sashes to be made of pine plank one inch and three quarters thick; the Lights to be of the best Crown Glass, eighteen in each Window, eleven inches by nine; the Window and Door Cases to be made with double Archatraves; and the lower Windows to have weights and pullies. The frame of the Roof to be of pine, except the King-Posts which are to be of oak; and the scantling to be of a size and proper proportion to the building. The Roof to be covered with inch pine plank well seasoned, and cyphered and lapt one inch and a half, and then with cypress shingles twenty inches long, and to show six inches. A Modillion Cornice on the outside, and a Cove Cornice on the inside, and the Roof to be framed according to the Plan thereof annexed.

"The Floors to be framed with good oak clear of sap, and laid with pine plank inch and a half thick, and well seasoned. The Ends of the Sleepers next the walls of the House to have at least six inches hold thereof, and their other ends next to the Isles to be supported by flush and entire brick walls or underpinning nine inches thick and of a proper height. The Isles to be laid with flaggstone, well squared and jointed.

"The Pews to be wainscoted with pine plank an inch and a half thick, well seasoned, to be quarter-round on both sides, and raised pannal on one

THE HISTORY OF TRURO PARISH

side; the seats to be of inch and half pine plank, fourteen inches broad and well supported. The Altar Piece to be twenty feet high and fifteen feet wide, and done with wainscot after the Ionic Order. the floor of the Communion Place to be raised twenty inches higher than the floor of the House, with hand-rails and Banisters of pine, and a Communion-Table of Black Walnut of a proper size. The Apostles Creed, the Lords-Prayer, and the ten Commandments to be neatly painted on the Altar-piece in black letters.

"The Pulpit, Canopy, and reading Desks to be of pine, wainscoted with proper Cornice, and executed in the Ionic Order.

"The inside of the Church to be Ceiled, Plaistered and White-Washed; no Loam or Clay to be used in the Plaistering. The Outside Cornice and all the Wooden-Work on the inside of the House (except the floors) to be neatly painted of the proper colours. Stone Steps to be put to the Doors, and locks and hinges; and hinges to the Pews, Pulpit and Communion Place.

"The whole Building to be compleated and finished by the first day of September, which shall be in the year of our Lord, One thousand seven hundred and seventy two, in a sufficient and workmanlike manner, and agreeable to the Plan thereof hereunto annexed, except with this Alteration in the West end of it, that instead of the door there shall be a window; and instead of the two windows, there shall be two doors opposite the two Isles.

"And the said Daniel French doth further agree to build two Horse-Blocks with each two flights of Steps; to fix six benches for the people to sit on under the trees; and to clear and remove all the rubbish and litter from off the Church Lott, so as to fit it for the Reception of the Congregation; and to have those additional works done by the time appointed for the finishing the Church.

"In Condition of the Premises the Vestry do agree to pay unto the said Daniel French the sum of Eight hundred and seventy seven pounds Current Money of Virginia in manner following, to wit, Two hundred pounds on the first day of September next; Two hundred and twenty-five pounds thirteen shillings and four pence on the first day of September, One thousand seven hundred and seventy; Two hundred and twenty five pounds thirteen shillings and four pence, on the first day of September, One thousand seven hundred and seventy one; and the remaining Two hundred and twenty five pounds thirteen shillings and four pence, on the first day of September, One thousand seven hundred and seventy two; at which time the Church is to be finished.

"In Witness whereof the said Parties, to wit, the Members of the said Vestry here present, and the said Daniel French, have hereunto Interchang-

THE HISTORY OF TRURO PARISH

ably set their Hands, the Day and Year first above written.

Signed and Delivered in the Presence of—	Danl. French
John Barry	Daniel Mc.Carty; C. W.
Wm. Triplett	Edwd. Payne
	Go. Washington
	Go. Wm. Fairfax
	Jno. Posey
	William Gardner
	Tz. Ellzey.

The next meeting of the Vestry was at Pohick Church, December 1, 1769. The Parish Levy provided for the payment,—To Mr. Daniel French for 3 acres and 26 perches of land laid off for the use of the Parish as per Plat, 4 Pounds, 2s. 4d. To Capt. Mc.Carty for advertising the letting of the Church, 18 shillings. For building the Church, &c. 34,900 pounds of Tobacco. Alexander Henderson and Thomas Ford appointed Church Wardens.

"Alexander Henderson, Gent. one of the Church Wardens for the ensuing year, and Augusus Darrell, having applied for the Collection of the Parish Levy, the said Augustus Darrell is appointed Collector, the Vestry being of opinion that it is improper for any member of the Vestry to be Collector of the Parish Levy. And it is ordered that the same be entered on the Records of this Parish; it having been heretofore customary that the

THE HISTORY OF TRURO PARISH

Church Wardens should have a preference of the collection to any other person."

Peirce Bayly's account as Collector and Sheriff was approved. It was "Ordered, that William Grayson Esqr. who has heretofore been appointed to prosecute suits for this Parish, be now appointed Attorney in fact for the Parish, and that he receive all Moneys and Tobacco arising from Fines and Judgments, and account with the Vestry annually for the same, at the laying of the Parish Levy."*

1770. Only one Vestry held, on November 28. Parish Levy included 56,330 pounds of tobacco for building the Church and as a fund for purchasing a Glebe. Honble. George William Fairfax Esqr. and Edward Payne, Gent. Church Wardens. Peter Wagener and Martin Cockburn, Gents. are elected Vestrymen in place of William Linton, deceased, and John Posey, removed. (These are the first breaks in the ranks of the Vestrymen elected in July, 1765.)

1771. July 8th. Messrs. Wagener and Cockburn subscribed the promise of conformity to the

---

*Among the duties of the Church Wardens was that of presenting to the Court of the County persons guilty of gambling, drunkenness, profanity, Sabbath breaking, failing to attend Church, disturbing public worship, and certain other offences against decency and morality. The fines imposed in these cases went to them for the use of the Parish, and are sometimes mentioned in the annual statement, though usually they would be included in the Wardens accounts which are not given in detail. That the Church Wardens of Truro, Cameron and Fairfax Parishes did not fail in this duty of presenting offenders is abundantly shown in records of the County Court. Presentments were usually made through the Grand Jury, the offender's Parish being designated, but sometimes the Church Wardens themselves are named as prosecutors.

THE HISTORY OF TRURO PARISH

doctrine and discipline of the Church of England, and were admitted as members of the Vestry. They, with Mr. Alex. Henderson, were added to those heretofore appointed to view and examine the new Church. Peirce Bayly, Collector, paid in fifty two hogsheads, 52,024 lbs. nett, of crop tobacco, and four transfer notes, gross 602 lbs. It was ordered to be sold in five lots, and the sale to be advertised in George Town, Alexandria, Dumfries and Colchester. 6 Pounds, 18s. and 8d. were allowed the Collector for prizing the tobacco.

"Whereas it appears that the dimensions of the Altar-piece mentioned in the Articles with the Undertaker for building the new Church, are not according to the proportions of Architecture, the Undertaker is authorized and desired to make the same according to the true proportions of the Ionic Order notwithstanding. And the Vestry being of the opinion that the stone coins are coarse grained and rather too soft they desire the same may be painted with white lead and oyle, which they think will make them sufficient. The Vestry are also of opinion that the rub'd bricks at the return of all the windows ought to be painted as near as possible the same colour with the arches, and the Undertaker is desired to do the same accordingly." November 29th. The Levy is laid as usual, and the Collectors and Church Wardens accounts exhibited and approved. Daniel French seems to have died since the last meeting, as payments are ordered made to his executor. It is seen later that his executor was Col. George Mason, by whom Pohick Church was completed. Rev. Lee Massey agreed to accept 50 Pounds in money in lieu of a Glebe, instead of the former 4,000 lbs. of tobacco. The same Processioners are appointed as four years before.

1772. June 5th. The Vestry being of opinion that it would be both ornamental and convenient to have the stone steps at the front door of the Church with three flights in place of only one in front, agreed to have them built in that manner, paying the difference in cost. The Church Wardens were ordered to agree with workmen to have the roof painted. Also for building a Vestry House of brick, twenty four by eighteen feet, nine feet pitch, plank floor, inside chimney and three windows.

"Ordered, that the six middle pews between the cross Isle and the Communion Table be sold for the benefit of the Parish, (one pew to be set up at a time,) to the highest bidder at the laying of the next Parish Levy, at six months credit, and that the Church Wardens and Vestry conduct the said sale and take proper bonds of the purchasers. And at the same time that the other six pews opposite them, on the other sides of the long Isles, be also sold to the highest bidder in like manner, or so many of them as will sell for the average price at which the first six pews shall be found to sell."

THE HISTORY OF TRURO PARISH

"The Church Wardens are directed to agree with persons to make such Carved Ornaments on the Altar piece as they shall judge proper, and guilding the letters thereon with Gold Leaf, presented to this Parish by the Honble. George Wm. Fairfax and George Washington Esqrs."

1772. November 20th. Alexander Henderson rendered his account, showing a balance of 460 Pounds, 5s. 7d. due the Parish. He is ordered to pay the Executors of Daniel French 225 Pounds, 13s. 4d., the last payment on the Church, and several other accounts due. Capt. Daniel Mc.Carty this day paid 330 Pounds, part of his bond for the Glebe land; which was lodged in the hands of Mr. Henderson, out of which he was to pay the proportion due to Fairfax Parish of the money for which the Glebe and Church plate sold, upon order of the Church Wardens who were to settle the account thereof with the Vestry of Fairfax Parish. The sum remaining unapplied was to be left in the hands of Mr. Henderson, he agreeing to pay interest on 150 Pounds thereof. The yard of the Upper Church was ordered inclosed with posts and rails, the posts to be split or sawed locust and the rails sawed. Also the steps and door sills to be repaired.

"The twelve pews ordered to be sold at the meeting of the last Vestry except the pew No. fifteen, were this day sold according to the said order, to the following persons, at the following prices, Vizt. No. three and No. four adjoining to the south wall of the Church, to Col. George Mason at the price of fourteen Pounds eleven shillings and eight pence each, being the average price at which the six pews first set up between the two long Isles and the Cross Isle sold. No. five adjoining the south wall above and next to front door to Mr. Thos. Withers Coffer, at the price of fourteen Pounds, thirteen shillings. No. thirteen adjoining the north wall, to Mr. Martin Cockburn, at the price of fifteen Pounds, ten shillings. No. fourteen adjoining to the north wall and next above the Rector's pew to Capt. Daniel Mc.Carty at the price of fifteen Pounds, ten shillings. No. twenty-one, being one of the six center pews adjoining the south Isle next to the Communion Table, to the Honble. George William Fairfax Esqr. at the price of sixteen pounds. No. twenty two and twenty three, two of the center pews adjoining the south Isle, to Mr. Alexander Henderson, Vizt. No. twenty two at the price of thirteen pounds, and No. twenty-three, next to the Cross Isle, at the price of thirteen pounds ten shillings. No. twenty eight, one of the Center pews adjoining the north Isle and next to the Communion Table, to Colo. George Washington at the price of sixteen pounds. No. twenty nine, one of the Center pews adjoining the north Isle, to Mr. Lund Washington, at the price of thirteen pounds ten shillings. No. thirty one of the Cen-

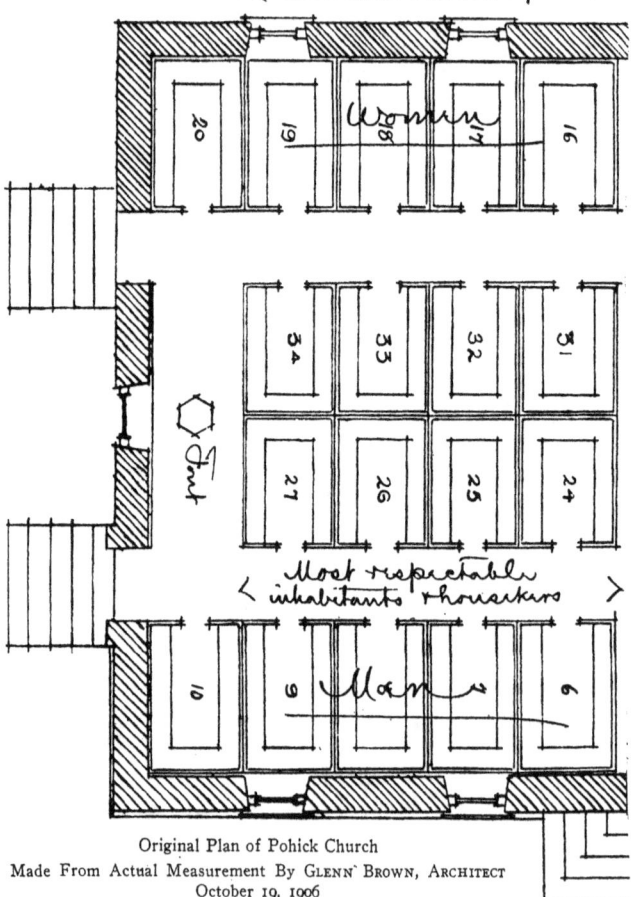

Original Plan of Pohick Church
Made From Actual Measurement By Glenn Brown, Architect
October 19, 1906

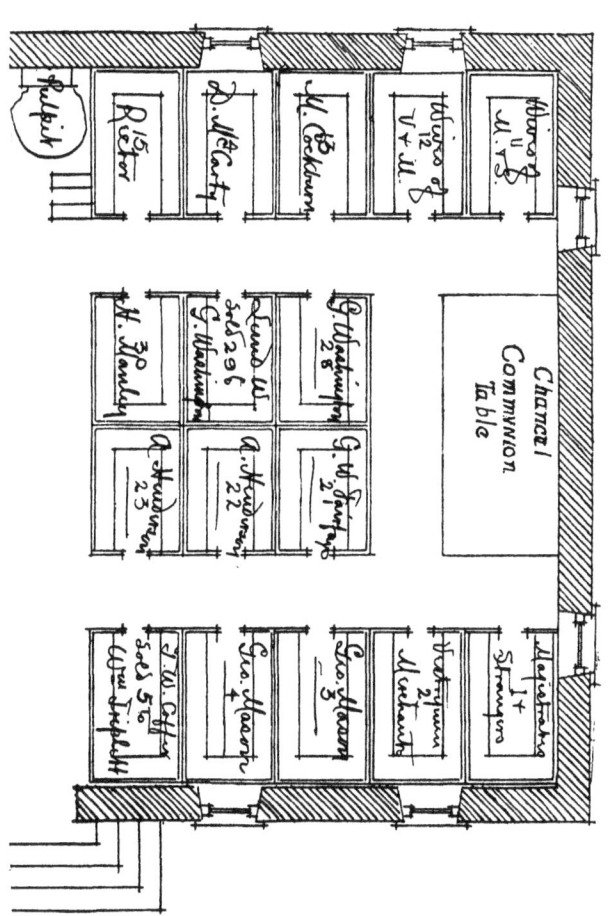

THE HISTORY OF TRURO PARISH

ter pews, adjoining the Center Isle and next the Cross Isle, to Mr. Harrison Manley at the price of fifteen pounds, ten shillings. It is ordered that the Church Wardens take the bonds for the use of the Parish, for the above mentioned purchase money, from the several respective purchasers, according to the order at the last Vestry; and that legal Deeds for the said Pews be made and executed by the Vestry to the said Purchasers for their Pews at the next meeting of the Vestry; the said purchasers preparing Deeds for that purpose."

"Ordered, that the Pew No. fifteen, adjoining to the North Wall of the Church and next above the pulpit, (which was one of the twelve pews ordered to be sold at the last Vestry, but is not sold,) be reserved for the Rector of this Parish for the Time being and his Family, and is hereby vested in the Rector of the Parish and his successors accordingly."

1773. June 4th. At a Vestry held for Truro Parish at the new Church at Pohick,—A Trust Deed for the pew above described, to the Rev. Lee Massey "for the use of himself and his Successors Rectors of this Parish forever, was this day executed by all the Members present, pursuant to an order of the Vestry made the 20th. day of November last."

"It appearing to the Vestry that the two lower pews between the two West doors are erected where the Font ought to be, it is ordered that

THE HISTORY OF TRURO PARISH

the said two pews be taken down and the space left open."

"Upon the Motion of the Honble. George William Fairfax Esqr. and Alexander Henderson, Gent. in behalf of themselves and the other purchasers of the six upper middle pews above the Cross Isle, leave is granted to the said purchasers to take up the stones in the Isles and to raise the said six pews at their own private expence to the same height above the Isles and exactly in the same manner with the pews next to the Walls, they making good any Damage that may happen in doing the same; and it is also ordered that the eight middle pews below the Cross Isles be raised in the same manner at the expence of the Parish."

"William Copein having undertaken to make a Stone Font for the Church according to a draught in the 150th. plate in Langleys Designs being the uppermost on the left hand for the price of six pounds he finding himself everything, the Vestry agree to pay him that sum for finishing the same."

November 22d. The parish Levy was laid and accounts rendered. Alex. Henderson has 218 pounds, thirteen shillings and ten pence half penny in his hands belonging to the Parish. He is ordered to pay William Copein seven pounds, five shillings for a stone Font and Step. George Mason and Edward Payne, Gents. appointed Church Wardens.

1174. February 15th. "George Mason, Esqr.

THE HISTORY OF TRURO PARISH

Executor of Daniel French decd. Undertaker of the Church near Pohick, having finished the said Church, tender(ed) the same to this Vestry (consisting of six members and the Rector of the Parish, besides the said George Mason,) and the said Vestry, being of opinion that the said Church is finished according to agreement do receive the same as far as they have authority to do so, the said George Mason undertaking to finish the Horse Blocks and Benches under the Trees, which was part of the original Agreement of the Undertaker. The said George Mason having produced his account against the Parish for extra work about the Church, the settlement of the same is referred to the next meeting of the Vestry." There were present, Lee Massey, R. T. P.; G. Mason, C. W.; Go. Washington, Daniel Mc.Carty, Alex. Henderson, Tz. Ellzey, Pet. Wagener, Martin Cockburn.

"At a Vestry held for Truro Parish at the new Church near Pohick, February the 24th. 1774.

"The receiving of the new Church near Pohick by an order of the last Vestry is confirmed, and the Executors of Mr. Daniel French deceased are discharged from their Testators Bond, upon finishing the Horse Blocks and Benches mentioned in the said order.

"George Mason Esqr. Executor of Daniel French decd. having exhibited an account amounting to the sum of one hundred and sixteen pounds nineteen shillings and ten pence halfpenny Curr. Money, for sundrie Alterations in the said Church and other work done thereto not inserted in the Undertakers Articles; the said account being sworn to by Going Lamphier, William Copein and William Bernard Sears was examined and approved; and it is ordered that Mr. Alexander Henderson pay him (out of the Parish's money in his hands) the sum of Fifty six pounds sixteen shillings and six pence halfpenny, being the balance due on the said account, after deducting the sum of twenty nine pounds three shillings and four pence for the price of two Pews in the said Church purchased by the said George Mason, and also thirty one pounds paid him by Capt. Daniel Mc.Carty and Mr. Martin Cockburn for their Pews.

"The Trust Deed from the Vestry to the Revd. Lee Massey for a Pew in the new Church dated June the 4th. 1773, not having been admitted to Record within the time limited by Law, the same is cancelled, and a new deed executed to him for the same Pew.

"Deeds were this day executed by the Vestry to the following Persons Vizt. George William Fairfax, George Mason and George Washington Esqr., Messrs. Daniel Mc.Carty, Alexander Henderson, Martin Cockburn, William Triplett, and John Manley Heir at Law of Harrison Manley decd., for the several Pews in the new Church

THE HISTORY OF TRURO PARISH

near Pohic bought by them at Public Auction the twentieth day of November 1772. The Pew then bought by Mr. Lund Washington being afterwards sold by him to the said George Washington, & the Pew then bought by Mr. Thomas Withers Coffer being afterwards sold by him to Mr. William Triplett, are conveyed by the Vestry accordingly.*

"Ordered, that the Upper Pew in the new Church adjoining the South Wall be appropriated to the Use of the Magistrates and Strangers, and the Pew opposite thereto to the use of their Wives, and the two Pews next below them to be appropriated to the Vestrymen and Merchants and their Wives in like manner. And it is further ordered that the eight Pews below and adjoining the Cross Isle of the Church be assigned to the use of the most respectable Inhabitants and House Keepers of the Parish, the Men to sit in the four pews next the South Wall, and the Women in the other four next the North Wall.

"The Church Wardens having failed to let the building of a Vestry House at the new Church pursuant to a former order of this Vestry, and the Vestry being now of opinion that it will be to the Advantage of the Parish to let the inclosing of the Church Yard together with the building of the said Vestry House, Ordered that the Vestry be

---
*A copy of the deed for the pews purchased by Washington will be found in the Appendix.

THE HISTORY OF TRURO PARISH

called to meet on Fryday the 22d. of April in order to let the building the said Vestry House and inclosing the said Church Yard, which inclosure is to be made of Brick one hundred and sixty feet square from out to out, three feet six inches high at the highest Part of the Ground, two Bricks thick, to go one foot below the surface and to be covered with Cypress Shingles and Painted, to have three Pier Gates. The Church Wardens to advertise the above meeting in the Virginia and Maryland Gazette after the usual Form upon such Occasions.

"Ordered that the new Church near Pohic be furnished with a Cushion for the Pulpit and Cloths for the Desks & Communion Table of Crimson Velvett with Gold Fring, and that Colo. George Washington be requested to import the same, as also two Folio Prayer Books covered with blue Turkey Leather with Name of the Parish thereon in Gold Letters, the Demensions of the said Cushion and Cloths being left to Wm. Bernard Sears who is desired to furnish Colo. Washington with proper Patterns at the Expense of the Parish."

"Lee Massey, R. T. P.   Alex. Henderson
G. Mason, C. W.   T. Ellzey
Edwd. Payne, C. W.   Thos. W. Coffer
G. Washington   Thos. Ford
Daniel Mc.Carty   Pet. Wagener
                         Martin Cockburn.
  "Recorded by John Barry, Clk. V."

THE HISTORY OF TRURO PARISH

(The above is an exact copy of the Records of this meeting.)*

The Vestry met again on February 25th. by adjournment from yesterday.

"Bonds being taken yesterday from Colo. George Washington for himself, and also as Attorney in Fact for Colo. George William Fairfax now in Brittain, from Mr. Alexander Henderson, Mr. William Triplett, and Mr. Thomas Triplett Executor of Harrison Manley decd. for the purchase Money of the Pews bought by them in the new Church near Pohick, the same Bonds were delivered to Colo. George Mason Church Warden to be by him collected and accounted for at the next laying the Levy, he having already received of Capt. Daniel Mc.Carty and Mr. Martin Cockburn the Price of their Pews purchased at the same time, which together with the Price of his own two Pews are deducted out of his account settled and received yesterday by the Vestry." William Bernard Sears was paid fifty eight pounds

---

*This was Washington's last Vestry. He continued a nominal Vestryman until 1782, but from this time his public duties took him from home, frequently at first and afterwards for many years continuously. Under date of July 10, 1783, he writes to his old friend, George William Fairfax, in London: "I have not been in the State (Virginia) but once since the 4th. of May, 1775. and that was at the seige of York. In going thither I spent one day at my own house, and in returning I took 3 or 4, without attempting to transact a particle of private business."

The regularity of Washington's attendance at the meetings of the Vestry is deserving of special notice. During the eleven years of his active service, from February, 1763, to February, 1774, thirty-one "Vestries" were held, at twenty-three of which he is recorded as being present. On the eight occasions when he was absent, as we learn from his Diary or other sources, once he was sick in bed, twice the House of Burgesses, of which he was a member, was in session, and three other times certainly, and on the two remaining occasions probably, he was out of the County.

nineteen shillings for carved work done by him in the new Church. William Copein was paid for extra work on the same Church, and Francis Coffer for railing the yard and making stone steps at the upper Church, and Gowan Langfier and Wm. Copein for their trouble and attendance in measuring the carved work on the Altar piece and Pulpit, the former thirty, the latter ten, shillings.

"Ordered that William Bernard Sears gild the Ornaments within the Tabernacle Frames, the Palm Branch and Drapery on the front of the Pulpit, (also the Eggs on the Cornice of the small Frames if the Gold will hold out,) which he agreed to do for three pounds ready money, to be done with the Gold Leaf given to the Parish by Colo. George Washington."

"The Vestry having reconsidered their order of yesterday directing the Church Yard to be inclosed with Brick, And considering that the expence thereof will be too burthensome to the Parish at this time having just finished two expensive Churches, and a Glebe not yet purchased, have changed their opinions, and do accordingly order that (instead of a Brick Wall) the said Church Yard be inclosed with a Post and Rail Fence in the following manner, to wit, with sawed Cedar Posts to go two feet and a half in the ground, to be first burnt, sawed Yellow Pine Rails clear of sap, five feet high from the surface to the top rail, Posts eight feet asunder, the whole to be well

THE HISTORY OF TRURO PARISH

payed with turpentine and red paint, with three Palisadoed Gates painted a Stone Colour with Locks."

The roof and fence at the Upper Church were ordered painted.

Capt. Edward Payne resigned as Vestryman, and Mr. Thomas Pollard was chosen in his stead.

1774. November 24th. The Parish Levy is laid, and accounts audited. George Washington Esqr. and Thomas Pollard Gent. are appointed Church Wardens for the next year. Alex. Henderson pays over to Mr. Pollard all money in his hands and is fully discharged of all accounts, and Col. Mason delivers to Mr. Pollard Col. George Washington's Bonds for his own pew and that of Col. Fairfax. Mr. Peter Wagener was chosen a Vestryman in the room of Major Peter Wagener, deceased.

1775. November 3d. The Levy shows 1363 tithables, as against 962 ten years before just after the division. This indicates the growth of the population. Col. Daniel Mc.Carty and Capt. Martin Cockburn were ordered to "take into their possession the books belonging to the Parish lately kept by John Barry, decd." The Revd. Lee Massey was appointed Clerk of the Vestry. Mr. Mason, Col. Mc.Carty, Capt. Cockburn, Capt. Pollard, Rev. Mr. Massey and Mr. Henderson were appointed to prepare a plan for the employment of

THE HISTORY OF TRURO PARISH

and providing for the poor of the Parish, and report to the next Vestry.

1776. May 6th. At the laying of the last Levy no Collector had been appointed, perhaps because none offered. On this day the Collection was let to the lowest bidder, agreeable to notice given, and was undertaken by William Bayly at nine per Cent. The regular price heretofore had been six per Cent. The Levy was very small, only twenty pounds per Poll.

1776. November 22d. Mr. Peter Wagener and Mr. Thomazen Ellzey appointed Church Wardens, and ordered to receive from former Wardens all balances due the Parish, including General George Washington's Bond and that of Col. George William Fairfax for which the General is liable, and to pay the several sums due the Parish Claimants charged this day, amounting to 119 pounds six shillings and four pence. William Triplett, Edward Ford and Francis Coffer were elected Vestrymen in the room of George William Fairfax Esqr. removed, Thomas Ford deceased, and William Gardner removed. The Church Wardens with Col. Mason and Capt. Cockburn, or any three of them, were appointed to look out for a tract of land suitable for a Glebe, and in case they succeeded were to report to a Vestry to be called for the purpose. The Levy was 30 pounds per Poll, on 1337 tithables. On the following April

THE HISTORY OF TRURO PARISH

William Payne the eldest undertook the collection at 8 per Cent.*

1777. October 2d. Deeds of Lease and Release from the Vestry to Col. Daniel Mc.Carty for the old Glebe were acknowledged by the Vestry, and the Church Wardens ordered to receive from Col. Mc.Carty the balance of the purchase money due. "Ordered, that the Church Wardens send Sarah Shelton (a poor child) to Dr. James of St. Mary's County Maryland and employ him to cure her of her present Disorders."

1777. November 27th. "William Triplett and Francis Coffer Gent. are appointed Church Wardens or Overseers of the Poor for the ensuing year." The Rev. Lee Massey resigned his office as Clerk of the Vestry, and Francis Adams was

---

*A special interest attaches to this levy because it was the last that was ever laid for the support of the old Colonial Church or the maintenance of religion in the Parish, such levies being from this time suspended by Act of Assembly and afterward abolished entirely. The support of the Clergy was left to be provided for by voluntary contributions.

There is no record of any effort being made for the future support of the Rev. Mr. Massey as Minister of this Parish. The disturbed condition of the times during the Revolution, and the absence of many leading men, may have prevented. Or more probably Mr. Massey wished to retire, for his Grandson, Col. J. T. Stoddert, of Maryland, wrote Bishop Meade that impaired speech was the cause of his ceasing to preach. After this he received for one year 500 pounds of tobacco as Clerk of the Vestry, and then his name disappears from the Records. We are told that he afterwards studied medicine and practised freely among the poor. He had been a practising lawyer before his ordination to the ministry, so it would seem that he followed successively what were known as the three learned professions of Law, Divinity and Medicine. He continued to live at "Bradley," his plantation on the Occoquan, until his death in 1814 at the age of eighty-six. A simple stone still marks his grave.

From this time forward the Records of the Vestry show their business to have been confined to the care of the poor, for which purpose levies of tobacco were still authorized. "Overseers of the Poor" became an alternate designation for the Church Wardens.

THE HISTORY OF TRURO PARISH

appointed in his stead. Tithables 1316. Levy 15 lbs. per Poll.

1778. No Levy was laid this year, as the Vestry found funds sufficient in their hands for the maintenance of the poor for the ensuing year.

1779. December 8th. Martin Cockburn Gent. having resigned his office as Vestryman Daniel Mc.Carty junior was elected in his stead, and Edward Washington junior was elected in place of Edward Ford who refused to serve. Tithables 1350. Levy 12 lbs. per Poll.

In 1780 no Vestry was held. November 27th, 1781, a Levy was laid of 10 lbs. per Poll, on 1442 Tithables. Daniel Mc.Carty and Thomazen Ellzey were appointed Church Wardens or Overseers of the Poor. William Deneale and Cleon Moore were elected Vestrymen in the room of Thomas Withers Coffer deceased and Daniel Mc.Carty junior who refused to act.

1782. November 22d. The Vestry met, and Daniel McCarty exhibited an account on oath against the Parish which showed it indebted to him in the sum of twelve pounds eight shillings paper money, which was ordered to be certified. Vestry adjourned until the 24th, but that meeting was not held.

1784. 23d February. The Vestry met at Colchester. "The Vestry of this Parish having appointed meetings at different times for two years last past, and not a majority of the said Vestry

THE HISTORY OF TRURO PARISH

meeting to proceed to business; It is now agreed upon and ordered that those of the Vestry who have resigned or removed others be chosen in their stead."

"John Gibson, Gent. is elected a Vestryman for this Parish in the room of His Excellency General Washington, who has signified his resignation in a letter to Daniel Mc.Carty, Gent."

James Waugh was elected in the room of Thomas Pollard, removed. Francis Coffer was desired to let the Vestry know at their next meeting whether he would continue to serve or not.

Peter Wagener and William Deneale were appointed Church Wardens or Overseers of the Poor. A Levy was laid, which included 10,000 lbs. of tobacco for the temporary support of such of the poor as are at present unknown, to be laid out by the Church Wardens at their discretion. This they considered "absolutely necessary on account of the severity of the winter and scarcity of corn."

Lund Washington was elected a Vestryman the room of Daniel Mc.Carty who now resigned. Present at this meeting:

Pet. Wagener, C. W.   Alex. Henderson.
W. Deneale, C. W.   Wm. Triplett.
G. Mason.   Edward Washington.
Daniel Mc.Carty.   Cleon Moore.*

---
*This meeting of the Vestry, which saw the formal **resignation** of George Washington, was the last that was attended by three of his friends and old fellow-Vestrymen, George Mason, Daniel Mc.-

THE HISTORY OF TRURO PARISH

The last meeting of the Vestry under the old *Regime* was held at Colchester, January 27th, 1785. Like the preceding it was occupied solely in providing for the support of the poor, and especially for twelve families who are named. The old Colonial Church, which had been staggering for years under blows inflicted by successive General Assemblies was now in the article of death. The leading men who, in the face of popular odium, stood by and attended it in its last hours, must have believed that when released from the coil of the State it would rise from the dust and put on more beautiful garments.

The new (Christ) Church in Alexandria had been finished about the same time with the new Pohick Church. Washington bought a pew in Christ Church on the day that the Church was turned over to the Vestry by the builders. He gave for Pew number 5, thirty six pounds, ten shillings. That pew has become historical. It was afterwards occupied by Gen. Robert E. Lee, and there are tablets on the walls of the Church in memory of these two heroic characters and devout Christians. This historic pew attracts every week streams of pilgrims to Christ Church.*

Carty and Alexander Henderson. Col. Mason and Capt. Mc.Carty were his seniors in point of service, having served continuously since 1749, a period of thirty-five years. Mr. Henderson was first elected on the new Vestry in 1765. The fifth and only remaining member of that Vestry, Mr. Thomazen Ellzey, was present at its last meeting two months later, and afterward continued to serve as an Overseer of the Poor.

*The pew which General Robert E. Lee rented and regularly occupied when at Arlington was across the aisle from **Washington's pew.**

THE HISTORY OF TRURO PARISH

Washington did not leave Pohick for Christ Church until after the Revolution, when services at the former became few and far between. April, 1785, seems to mark the date of his habitual attendance at Christ Church. On the 25th of that month he bound himself by a paper of record in the Vestry Book, signed in his well known handwriting, to pay an annual rent upon his pew. The structure of this bond indicates that it was Washington's composition. The following is a copy of it from the record:

"We, the subscribers, do hereby agree that the pews we now hold in the Episcopal Church at Alexandria shall be forever charged with an an-

---

On a fly leaf of Washington's diary for January, 1773, is the following memorandum:
"Sale of the pews in Alexandria Church—to whom—&ca.

Nos.	Purchasers	Price
4	Mr. Townsd. Dade	L 28
5	Colo. G. Washington	36.10
13	Mr. Robt. Adam	30
14	Mr. Robt. Alexander	30.10
15	Mr. Dalton	20
18	Mr. Thos. Fleming	21.5
19	Col. Carlyle	30
20	Mr. Wm. Ramsey	33
28	Messrs. Jno. Muir &ca.	36.5
29	Mr. Jno. West Junr.	33

L 298.10

Average price 29.17."

For some reason the Vestry of Fairfax Parish proposed to set aside the sale of these pews. Washington was informed by Capt. John Dalton when the meeting was to be held to determine the matter, and was invited to be present. In his letter to Capt. Dalton, dated 15th. February, 1773, he says: "I am obliged to you for the notice you have given me of an intended meeting of your Vestry on Tuesday next." He explains why he would not come to make his protest in person, and adds: "The right of reclaiming the pews by the Vestry in behalf of the Parish I most clearly deny. As a parishioner I protest against the measure. As a subscriber who meant to lay the foundation of a family pew I shall think myself injured:" etc., etc.

Washington was a "parishioner" of this parish by virtue of being a freeholder and tithe-payer therein. His protest seems to have had the desired effect, as he remained in possession of his pew.

THE HISTORY OF TRURO PARISH

nual rent of five pounds, Virginia money, each; and we hereby promise to pay (each for himself promising to pay) annually, forever, to the Minister and Vestry of the Protestant Episcopal Church in Fairfax Parish, or, if the Parish should be divided, to the Minister and Vestry of the Protestant Episcopal Church in Alexandria, the said sum of five pounds for each pew for the purpose of supporting the Minister in the said Church. Provided neverthelsss that if any law of this Commonwealth should hereafter compel us, our heirs, executors and administrators or assigns, to pay to the support of Religion, the pew-rent hereby granted shall, in that case, be considered as part of what we, by such law, be required to pay.

Provided also that each of us pay only in proportion to the part we hold of the said pews.

For the performance of which payments, well and truly to be made forever annually, within six months after demanded, we hereby bind ourselves (each for himself separately) our heirs, executors, administrators and assigns, firmly by these presents. In witness whereof, we have hereunto set our hands and seals this 25th day of April in the year of our Lord 1785.

Witness present at signing and sealing.
David Griffith at
signing and sealing for (Seal) Philip Alexander.
G. Washington, W. Bird   Robert Adams.
T. Herbert & P. Alexander.   M. Madden.

THE HISTORY OF TRURO PARISH

Giles Cooke for T. West.
Barr Powell for W. Herbert.
    Geo. Washington (Seal)
Gr. Chapman for R. Adams.
    W. Bird (Seal)
Robt. Macgill for M. Madden.
    Thos. Herbert (Seal)
    Thomas West (Seal)
    W. Herbert (Seal)

And yet Washington occasionally attended Pohick Church when it was open for Divine Service, as the following item from his Diary proves:

"Oct. 2d. 1785. Sunday. Went with Fanny Bassett, Burwell Bassett, Dr. Stuart, George A. Washington, Mr. Shaw and Nelly Custis to Pohick Church to hear a Mr. Thompson preach who returned home with us to dinner, where I found Rev. Mr. Jones, formerly a Chaplain in a Pa. Regiment. After we were in bed about eleven o'clock at night, Mr. Houdon (sent from Paris by Mr. Jefferson and Dr. Franklin to take my Bust, in behalf of the State of Virginia, with three young men, assistants, introduced by Mr. Perin a French gentleman of Alexandria) arrived here by water from the latter place. 3d. October. The two Reverend gentlemen who dined and lodged here went away after breakfast." This is an illustration of the truth of the statement of his Pastor, Rev. Lee Massey, that Washington never allowed company at Mount Vernon to keep him from Church, and

THE HISTORY OF TRURO PARISH

that he was the most punctual and constant attendant at Divine Service he had ever known. Mrs. Lewis, (Nelly Custis,) bears a like testimony as to his habit in New York and Philadelphia. As to the time of which we are now speaking she says: "General Washington had a pew in Pohick Church and one in Christ Church, Alexandria. He attended the Church at Alexandria when the weather and roads permitted a ride of ten miles."

We have reached the dark age of Truro Parish. There are no records to guide us, and we have to avail ourselves of such side-lights as come from other sources. It is not known definitely when Mr. Massey's official relations with the Parish ceased. Tradition says he was followed by a Mr. Kemp and a Mr. Moscrope, who did not walk worthy of their high vocation in several respects. Whether they had any official connection with the Parish, or were merely "temporary supplies," is not known.* Towards the close of the century, some say in 1798, the eccentric Mason L. Weems appears upon the scene. There is no proof of his precise relations to the Parish. In his popular Life of Washington he calls himself "Late Rector of Mount Vernon Parish," as if he did not know its name. It is certain however that he was officiating there about the beginning of this century. Mr.

---

*Bishop Meade, from whom this tradition was drawn, had heard that these Ministers "Occasionally officiated at Dumfries, Pohick, and perhaps at Centerville,'" (doubtless a slip of the pen for Brentsville). I do not find their names in any lists of the Clergy of that period.

THE HISTORY OF TRURO PARISH

Davis, a teacher in that section, published a work dedicated to Jefferson, and entitled, "Four and a Half Years in America." In it he says: "About eight miles from Occoquan Mills is a place of worship called Poheek (sic) Church. Thither I rode on Sunday and joined the congregation of Parson Weems, a Minister of the Episcopal persuasion, who was cheerful in his mein that he might win men to religion. A Virginian Churchyard on Sunday resembles rather a race-course than a sepulchral ground. The ladies come to it in carriages and the men make their horses fast to the trees. But the steeples of the Virginian Churches are designed not for utility but for ornament, for the bell is suspended from a tree.† It is also observable that the gate to the Churchyard is ever carefully locked by the Sexton, who retires last. I was confounded on first entering the Churchyard at Poheek to hear "Steed threaten Steed with high and boastful neigh." Nor was I less stunned with the rattling of carriage-wheels, the cracking of whips and the vociferations of the gentlemen to the Negroes who accompanied them. But the discourse of Parson Weems calmed every perturbation, for he preached the great doctrines of Salvation as one who had experienced their power. In his youth Mr. Weems had accompanied some young Americans to London where he prepared himself by dilligent study for the profession

---
†It is hard to determine what could have suggested this remark, as Pohick Church had neither bell nor steeple.

THE HISTORY OF TRURO PARISH

of the Church. Of the congregation about one half was composed of white people and the other of negroes. Among many of the negroes were to be discovered the most gratifying evidences of sincere piety, an artless simplicity, passionate aspirations after Christ and an earnest endeavour to do the will of God."

The light thus thrown by Mr. Davis upon Pohick Church for one Sunday reveals a very animated and picturesque scene, and one by no means discreditable to Mr. Weems. This single glimpse into the darkness which shrouded Truro Parish is the only authentic tidings we have of it until 1812, when the Rev. Charles O'Neill is in charge. We first meet Mr. O'Neill in St. Thomas' Parish, Orange County, where he officiated and taught school in 1797-1800. He was one of the old-time schoolmasters, (as we have seen in our History of St. Mark's Parish,) who believed in what Hudibras called "Apostolic blows and knocks" more than he did in the Apostolic Succession. His whipping post was the back of a negro man, on which the bad boy was suspended and flaggellated with hickory switches. He taught at Col. Taliaferro's, near Pine Stake Church, and also in Bromfield Parish, Madison County. Judge P. P. Barbour, of the U. S. Supreme Court, and the Hon. Jeremiah Morton and Dr. George Morton were his pupils, and retained a lively impression of his discipline. He also preached and taught school in Hamilton Par-

THE HISTORY OF TRURO PARISH

ish, Fauquier County, and represented it in Convention in 1805. He was likewise in Dettingen Parish, Prince William County. The date of his incumbency in Truro Parish was the time of Bishop Meade's effective ministry at Christ Church, Alexandria. The family at Mount Vernon were attendants at Christ Church at this time, and some of them were among the first fruits of his ministry there. Mr. Meade was consequently intimate at Mount Vernon, and tells an amusing anecdote of Mr. O'Neill. He says: "The family at Mt. Vernon and at Rippon Lodge (the Blackburns) were fond of him. He, (O'Neill,) always spent his Christmas at Mt. Vernon, and on those occasions was dressed in a full suit of velvet, which Gen. Washington had left behind, and which had been given to Mr. O'Neill. But as General Washington was tall and well proportioned in all his parts, and Mr. O'Neill was peculiarly formed, being of uncommon length of body and brevity of legs, it was difficult to make the clothes of the one, even though altered, sit well on the other." (Mr. O'Neill died, it is thought, in 1813.)

Judge Bushrod Washington, (the son of John A. and nephew of General Washington,) who inherited Mt. Vernon, was now living there. He was a devout Communicant of the Church, and attended Divine Service in Christ Church, Alexandria, which he represented repeatedly in convention. He was also a member of the Standing Com-

THE HISTORY OF TRURO PARISH

mittee to the end of his life. He married Jane, daughter of Col. Thomas Blackburn, of Rippon Lodge, Prince William County, which was a center of Episcopal influence. Two of the Misses Blackburn, Jane and Polly, married nephews of General Washington and lived in Jefferson County, and one, Judy, married Gustavus Alexander. The first Richard Blackburn married a daughter of the Rev. James Scott, of Overwharton Parish.

In his Convention Address in 1838 Bishop Meade thus describes a visitation made to Pohick Church, and its condition, in the preceding summer:

"My next visit was to Pohick Church, in the vicinity of Mt. Vernon, the seat of General Washington. It was still raining when I approached the house, and found no one there. The wide-open doors invited me to enter,—as they do invite, day and night through the year, not only the passing traveller, but every beast of the field and fowl of the air. These latter however seeemed to have reverenced the house of God, since few marks of their pollution were to be seen throughout it. The interior of the house, having been well built, is still good. The chancel, Communion table and tables of the law &c. are still there and in good order. The roof only is decaying; and at the time I was there the rain was dropping on these sacred places and on other parts of the house. On the doors of the pews, in gilt letters, are still to be

THE HISTORY OF TRURO PARISH

seen the names of the principal Families which once occupied them. How could I, while for at least an hour traversing those long aisles, ascending the lofty pulpit, entering the sacred chancel, forbear to ask, And is this the House of God which was built by the Washingtons, the Mc.Cartys, the Lewises, the Fairfaxes?—the house in which they used to worship the God of our fathers according to the venerable forms of the Episcopal Church,—and some of whose names are still to be seen on the doors of those now deserted pews? Is this also destined to moulder piecemeal away, or, when some signal is given, to become the prey of spoilers, and to be carried hither and thither and applied to every purpose under heaven?

"Surely patriotism, or reverence for the greatest of patriots, if not religion, might be effectually appealed to in behalf of this one temple of God. The particular location of it is to be ascribed to Washington, who, being an active member of the Vestry when it was under consideration and in dispute where it should be placed, carefully surveyed the whole parish, and, drawing with his own hand an accurate and handsome map of it, showed clearly where the claims of justice and the interests of religion required its erection.

"It was to this Church that Washington for some years regularly repaired, at a distance of six or seven miles, never permitting any company to prevent the regular observance of the Lord's day.

THE HISTORY OF TRURO PARISH

And shall it now be permitted to sink into ruin for want of a few hundred dollars to arrest the decay already begun? The families that once worshipped there are indeed nearly all gone, and those who remain are not competent to its complete repair. But there are immortal beings all around it, and not far distant from it, who might be forever blessed by the word faithfully preached therein. The poor shall never cease out of any land, and to them the gospel ought to be preached.

"For some years past one of the students in our Theological Seminary has acted as lay reader in it, and occasionally a professor has added his services. Within the last year the Rev. Mr. Johnson, residing in the neighbourhood, has performed more frequent duties there.

"On the day following I preached to a very considerable congregation in this old church, one third of which was made up of coloured persons. The sacrament was then administered to twenty persons."

Some years later the Bishop wrote: "I am happy to say that this report led the Rev. Mr. Johnson to its use, in a circular, by means of which he raised fifteen hundred dollars, with which a new roof and ceiling and other repairs were put on it, by which it has been preserved from decay and fitted for such occasional services as are performed there. A friend, who has recently visited it, informs me that many of the doors of the pews are

THE HISTORY OF TRURO PARISH

gone. Those of George Washington and George Mason are not to be found,—perhaps borne away as relics. Those of George William Fairfax, Martin Cockburn, Daniel Mc.Carty, William Payne, (read Triplett,) and the rector's, are still standing and their names legible."

Alexander Henderson

This gentleman was the son of Rev. Robert Henderson, Minister of Blantyre in Scotland. He came to Virginia in 1756, and settled as a merchant in Colchester, in Truro Parish. He married Miss Sallie Moore of Maryland. His son, General Henderson, says that during the Revolution he retired to a farm in Fairfax County for fear of falling into the hands of the English, as he had taken a very decided part against the mother-country. He, General Washington and George Mason, were commissioners on the part of Virginia who met with the Maryland commissioners, Stone, Chase and Jenifer, at Mount Vernon on the 28th of March, 1785, made the compact as to the navigation and exercise of jurisdiction in the waters of Chesapeake Bay and Pocomoke. Col. Henderson represented Prince William County in the General Assembly in 1798, having in the meantime moved to Dumfries, which had long been one of the chief marts of commerce in Virginia. The late Murray Forbes, of Falmouth, son of Dr. Stirling Forbes, an eminent physician of Dumfries, when a boy became one of his clerks, living in his family and sharing his kindness with his sons. Col. Henderson established a branch of his business in Alexandria in connection with his cousin and son-in-law, known as "Scotch Sandy." In process of time he sent Mr. Forbes to Alexandria to manage his share in the firm. When Mr. Forbes had become of age Col. Henderson told him he would like to keep him in his service, as he had conducted his business to his satisfaction and to his own credit. But he added, "You should go into business on your own account. Here is a check for $5000 in compensation for your services, and I will give you a letter of credit for $5000 more. Mr. Forbes was overwhelmed with surprise at the proposition, but the Colonel insisted, and Mr. Forbes became the accomplished merchant and gentleman so well known in Falmouth. He cherished a profound homage for Col. Henderson's memory, and told his eldest son to hold his name, character and lineage, in high respect. Col. Henderson died in 1815, leaving six sons and four daughters. John, Alexander and James moved to Wood County, West Va. Richard was an eminent lawyer of Leesburg. Archibald was Gen. Henderson of the Marine Corps, U. S. A. Thomas was a distinguished Surgeon of the Army, and one of the founders of the Theological Seminary of Virginia. One of his daughters, Sarah, was a devout and sweet poetess, and married Gen. Francis H. Smith, the Superintendent of the Virginia Military Institute. This old Vestryman is now represented in the Parish by one of his lineal descend-

THE HISTORY OF TRURO PARISH

ants, Mrs. Dr. Nevitt, of Accotink, who, like her great grandfather, worships in the same old Pohick Church.

LUND WASHINGTON, who became a Vestryman in 1782, was the son of Townshend Washington and Elizabeth Lund, of Chotank Creek, King George County. He was born October 1, 1737, and died in 1796. In his youth he was a manager of a large estate in Albemarle and Orange. He was then appointed manager of Ravensworth in Fairfax by Col. Henry Fitzhugh, of King George. Subsequently he was chosen by General Washington to superintend Mt. Vernon, which he did until 1785. He was a man of great bodily strength and activity, and made money for his employers and for himself. He married his cousin, Betsey Foote.

EDWARD WASHINGTON was chosen Vestryman in 1779. Lund Washington says of him: "Edward Washington lived a few miles from Colchester when I went there to live in 1786. My uncle, Lawrence Washington and I believed him to be a relative from his strong resemblance to the family." His father was living in 1788, a very old man.

DR. PETER WAGENER, Vestryman in 1771, was an Englishman, and was Clerk of Stafford County before Fairfax was established. It was on his land that the town of Colchester was founded in 1754, and he was one of the original Trustees

THE HISTORY OF TRURO PARISH

with Daniel Mc.Carty, John Barry, William Elzy and Edward Washington. He married a sister of Mr. Speaker Robinson of the House of Burgesses. (1750.) Their daughter Elizabeth married Rev. Spence Grayson of Dettingen Parish, (1781-1797). Peter Wagener, son of the foregoing, was chosen Vestryman in 1774 to succeed his father who died that year. He was Clerk of Fairfax County, and married a daughter of Daniel Mc.-Carty. Their son, Beverly Robinson, married in 1790 a daughter of Col. Benjamin Harrison of Prince William County. A daughter of Peter Wagener married Dr. Morton of Colchester, and 2d. Col. Porter of Prince William.

LAWRENCE LEWIS, of Woodlawn, was the son of Col. Fielding Lewis, of Fredericksburg, and his wife Betty, only sister of General Washington. He was born April 4, 1767. Col. Fielding Lewis, by his last will, dated October 19, 1781, devised to his son Lawrence one thousand acres of land in the County of Frederick, one sixth of his negroes and one third of his stock of cattle, horses, &c. When Lawrence had attained the age of twenty one he was engaged by his uncle to live at Mt. Vernon and aid him in receiving strangers and entertaining the perpetual flow of company to that hospitable mansion. In his letter Gen. Washington said:—"Your Aunt and I are in the decline of life and are regular in our habits, especially of rising and going to bed. I require some fit person to ease me of the trouble of entertaining company, particularly of nights, it being my inclination to retire, and, (unless prevented by very particular company,) I always do retire either to bed or to my study, soon after candle light. In taking these duties, which hospitality always obliges me to bestow upon company, off my hands, it would render me a very acceptable service."

Mt. Vernon was the home of the beautiful Nellie Custis, Mrs. Washington's grauddaughter, when Lawrence Lewis entered the bower. Two such bright particular stars thus moving in the same orbit, by a mutual attraction soon became one, according to that saying of our quaint old South,—"An invisible hand from Heaven mingles hearts by a strange secret and unaccountable conjunction."

Gen. Washington in his last will devises two thousand acres of the Mt. Vernon estate to Lawrence Lewis and his wife, Eleanor P. (Custis) Lewis. The writer has a beautiful plot of this land, with endorsement: "A Plan of a part of Mt. Vernon lands, N. W. of the road leading from the gum spring on little Hunting Creek to the ford of Dogue Run. Beginning at three red marked oaks on a rising therein, opposite to the old road which formerly passed through the S. end of Muddy Hole farm, including that part of Chaple land which belongs to the subscriber, as also the Mill and Distillery, showing the slopes, contents and relative

THE HISTORY OF TRURO PARISH

situation of every field, lot, meadow, and likewise the shape and contents of every piece of woodland appertaining thereto; the whole having been laid down by an actual and accurate survey, Sept. 20, 1799.

G. Washington."

This survey was Washington's work less than three months before his death.

COL. WILLIAM GRAYSON. This gentleman, spoken of in the Records as the Attorney for the Vestry, merits special mention. He was the son of Benjamin Grayson, a wealthy merchant of Colchester, who married Susan Monroe of Westmoreland. He was the brother of Rev. Spence Grayson, Rector of Dettingen Parish. William Grayson, born 1736, was educated in England and practiced law in Dumfries. On 11th of November, 1774, the Independent Company of Cadets was formed in Prince William and chose Grayson their Captain. The motto of the Company, was, *"Aut Liber aut Nullus."* A Committee consisting of Philip R. F. Lee was sent to wait on Col. Washington and ask him to take command of the Company as Field Officer. To this he assented, and when he took command of the Army he took leave of them in a formal letter. This Company offered to unite with the Fredericksburg Company and march to Williamsburg.

Grayson was often at Mt. Vernon, as stated in

THE HISTORY OF TRURO PARISH

Washington's Diary. In August, 1776, Washington appointed him one of his Aids, and he was with him in many campaigns in New Jersey and New York, distinguishing himself by his gallantry at Monmouth, and was in hearing of the spicy colloquy between Gen. Washington and Gen. Charles Lee. Grayson and Lieut. Col. Jones were appointed Colonels of the two new Regiments raised in Virginia. He was put by Washington at the head of a Commission to settle the vexed questions arising out of the capture of Gen. Charles Lee. In 1778 he was made Commissioner on the Board of War. Bishop White used to tell an anecdote of the bold and dashing way in which he, at this time, dispersed a mob near his house in Philadelphia. In 1784 he was elected to Congress, and also made a member of a Court for determining a dispute between Massachusetts and New York. In 1778 he was a member of the Virginia Convention to consider the ratification of the Constitution of the United States, and spoke and voted against it, chiefly upon the ground that the proposed Constitution would destroy the rights of the States, and there were no adequate checks against the abuse of power, especially by the President, who was responsible only to his counsellors and partners in crime, the members of the Senate. And yet, though in the minority on this exciting question, he and Richard Henry Lee were chosen the first Senators in Congress from Virginia. He

THE HISTORY OF TRURO PARISH

served one session in the Senate, and died on his way to the second, on the 12th of March, 1790, and was buried in the family vault at Belaire in Prince William County. Although Col. Grayson filled so many public trusts with signal ability, he has, from want of a biographer, almost lapsed from history, while other inferior men live in story and song. In person he was six feet high, of a full habit and florid complexion, with black hair and eyes. With his varied culture he was elegant in conversation as he was able in debate. He married a sister of Gen. Smallwood, of Maryland, and left four sons, William, George, Alfred and Robert, and one daughter, Helen, who married John Carter, of Loudoun, who went to Kentucky, and whose eldest son moved to Tennessee. Robert married Miss Breckenridge, of Kentucky.

GEORGE JOHNSTON. This gentleman, one of the legal advisers of the Vestry, was the son of Dr. James Johnston who migrated to Maryland. The son came to Virginia and settled in Fairfax County, which he represented in the General Assembly. Patrick Henry's famous resolutions were seconded by Mr. Johnston in a "speech of great eloquence and power." He married Miss Thompson, by whom he had two daughters, one of whom married Rev. Lee Massey, of Truro Parish, and the other married Robert Howson Harrison, one of Washington's aids. He married for his second wife Miss Mc.Carty, by whom he had five sons and

THE HISTORY OF TRURO PARISH

four daughters. Two of his sons were officers in the Revolution, and a grandson, Major George Johnston, in the Confederate States Army.

MARTIN COCKBURN, whose name so often appears in the Parish Records, was a native of Jamaica. While travelling in Virginia, in his eighteenth year, with Dr. Cockburn, he became fascinated with Miss Bronaugh. She would not go to Jamaica, and he had to come to Virginia to win the prize. He bought a farm, Springfield, near Gunston, where they lived to a good old age. He was a polished Christian gentleman, much esteemed by George Mason, as is attested by their correspondence still extant.

CAPT. CLEON MOORE, of Colchester, elected Vestryman in 1781, was badly wounded at the battle of Brandywine. He moved to Alexandria in 1800 and was appointed Register of Wills, which office he filled until his death in 1808. He was succeeded by his son Alexander, who was born at Colchester January 8, 1786. His first wife was the daughter of Col. Roger West, of West Grove, Fairfax County. Cleon Moore was the author of Washington's March. He was wont to tell this anecdote of himself, says Mr. Brocket, of the "Lodge of Washington":

During the Revolution he was stationed with a squad of men in the Northern Neck, without rations. Chancing to see a flock of geese, belonging to a Mr. Page, he "impressed" them, except a

THE HISTORY OF TRURO PARISH

gander, to whose neck he attached a piece of paper, containing nine-pence, with these lines:—

> "My good Mr. Page,
> Be not in a rage,
> Nor think it a very great wonder;
> We have taken nine geese,
> At a penny apiece,
> And sent the money home by the gander."

[END OF DR. SLAUGHTER'S MANUSCRIPT.]

THE HISTORY OF TRURO PARISH

THOMAS WITHERS COFFER, born 1713, and a Vestryman of Truro from 1765 to his death, in 1781, was a son of Francis Coffer, (born 1683, died 1740) and Mary Littlejohn Withers, his wife. His seat was at or near the present residence of M. D. Hall, Esq., whose wife is one of his descendants; so he was one of the "upper" Vestrymen, being a neighbor, as neighbors were accounted then, of Capt. Payne, Mr. Gardner, Mr. Ford and Mr. Ellzey. His wife was Mary Ferguson, who was born in 1715 and died in 1758. Their son Francis Coffer was born in 1748, and was a Vestryman from 1776 to 1785. He married a Miss Gunnell. Thomas Coffer, their son, born 1773, was captain of a company from Fairfax in the war of 1812. He married Ann Simpson, and died in 1862, leaving eight children, namely: William Coffer, married Miss Harmed, line extinct; Hannah Coffer, married Silas Burke; Jane Coffer, married Levi Burke; Elizabeth Coffer, married George Selectman; Thomas Coffer, married Jane Selectman; Henry Coffer, married Harriett Taylor; Joshua Coffer, married Hulda Simpson; Armistead Thompson Mason Coffer, died unmarried. The descendants of Hannah, Jane, Henry and Joshua Coffer have restored a pew in Pohick Church in memory of Thomas Withers Coffer.

TRIPLETT. The will of Francis Triplett of the Parish of Truro is dated October 4th, 1757, and gives the names of his children, Thomas, Wil-

THE HISTORY OF TRURO PARISH

liam, Daniel, John, Francis, Mason, Margaret (married Boylston,) and Patty. Of these William Triplett was a Vestryman of Truro from 1776 to 1785, being elected in the room of George William Fairfax. He was a man of prominence in his neighborhood, and was among the friends invited by Mrs. Washington to the funeral of the General. Thomas Triplett was a trooper in the French and Indian War, March, 1756; and his brother Francis Triplett was in Col. George Washington's regiment in the same war. The latter received a wound in the arm, for which 55 pounds was granted him by the General Assembly. He was afterward a captain of militia in Fauquier County, a Justice of the Peace and a Vestryman of Leeds Parish. His daughter Ann married Capt. Elias Hord. The Rev. Arnold H. Hord, of Philadelphia, is among her descendants.

VESTRYMEN AND CHURCH WARDENS OF TRURO
PARISH. 1732-1785.
(C. W.=Church Warden.)

Dennis Mc.Carty, 1732-41.
John Heryford, 1732-43 died. C. W. 1732-4.
Edward Barry, 1732-44. C. W. 1737-44.
Charles Broadwater, 1732-33 and 1744-65. C. W. 1750-1, 52-3, 56-7.
Richard Osborne, 1732-48. C. W. 1747-8.
John Lewis, 1732-33.
Gabriel Adams, 1732-33.
Edward Emms, 1732-48. C. W. 1732-6, 48-9.
Francis Awbrey, 1733-34.
William Godfrey, 1733-44.
John Sturman, 1733-46. C. W. 1743.
Giles Tillett, 1733-34.
Rev. Lawrence De Butts, Minister, 1733-34.
Michael Ashford, 1733-34.
Jeremiah Bronaugh, 1733-44, and 1747-50 died. C. W. 1734-7, 42-4, 48.
William Peake, 1733-44, and 1749-62 died.
John Farguson, 1733-44.
Thomas Lewis, 1733-44. C. W. 1736-40.
James Baxter, 1734-36.

THE HISTORY OF TRURO PARISH

John Colvill, 1734-48. C. W. 1740-2.
Augustine Washington, 1735-37.
Rev. Charles Green, Rector, 1737-64.
John Baxter, 1743-44.
Robert Boggess, 1744-65. C. W. 1748-9, 54-5, 59-61.
Daniel French, 1744-46.
Andrew Hutchinson, 1744-48. C. W. 1747-8.
John Minor, 1744-48. C. W. 1746-7.
Lewis Ellzey, 1744-48, and 1765. C. W. 1744-6.
John West, 1744-48, and 1750-65. C. W. 1744-6, 55-8.
Hugh West, 1744-54 died. C. W. 1746-7, 48.
George Mason, 1749-85. C. W. 1750, 55-6, 65-6, 73-4.
Daniel Mc.Carty, 1749-84. C. W. 1751-2, 53-4, 58-9, 64-5, 68-9, 75-6, 78-9, 81-4.
John Turley, 1749-56. C. W. 1754-5.
James Hamilton, 1749-56. C. W. 1750-1.
William Payne, Sr., 1750-65. C. W. 1751-2, 57-8.
Abraham Barnes, 1750-65. C. W. 1753-4, 59-61.
William Fairfax, 1754-57 died.
William Payne, Jr., 1756-65. C. W. 1761-3, 64.
Henry Gunnell, 1756-65. C. W. 1761-3.
George William Fairfax, 1757-76. C. W. 1763-4, 70-1.

THE HISTORY OF TRURO PARISH

George Washington, 1762-65, and 1765-84. C. W. 1763-4, 66-7, 74-5.

Edward Payne, 1765-74. C. W. 1765-6, 70-1, 73-4.

Thos. Withers Coffer, 1765-84 died. C. W. 1768-9, 71-2.

William Gardner, 1765-76. C. W. 1766-7.

Alexander Henderson, 1765-85. C. W. 1769-70, 79-80.

Thomazen Ellzey, 1765-85. C. W. 1767-8, 72-3, 76-7, 81-4.

Thomas Ford, 1765-76. C. W. 1769-70.

John Ford, 1765.

Peter Wagener, Sr., 1765, 72-74 died. C. W. 1771-2.

William Linton, 1765-70 died.

John Posey, 1765-70. C. W. 1767-8.

Rev. Lee Massey, Rector, 1767-77.

Martin Cockburn, 1770-79. C. W. 1772-3.

Thomas Pollard, 1774-84. C. W. 1774-6, 78-9.

Peter Wagener, Jr., 1774-85. C. W. 1776-7, 79-80, 84-5.

William Triplett, 1776-85. C. W. 1777-8.

Francis Coffer, 1776-85. C. W. 1777-8.

Edward Washington, 1779-85.

William Deneale, 1781-85. C. W. 1784-5.

Cleon Moore, 1781-85.

John Gibson, 1784-85.

James Waugh, 1784-85.

Lund Washington, 1784-85.

THE HISTORY OF TRURO PARISH

All Vestries were dissolved at Easter, 1785, by the Act of Assembly by which the Protestant Episcopal Church was incorporated.

CLERKS OF THE VESTRY

Edward Barry, 1732-44.
William Henry Terrett, 1744-56.
John West, Jr., 1756-64.
John Barry, 1764-75.
Rev. Lee Massey, 1775-77.
Francis Adams, 1777-79.
Peter Wagener, 1781-85.

CLERKS AND LAY READERS AT THE CHURCHES

Joseph Johnson, New, or Falls, and Goose Creek, 1733-35.
Edward Barry, Pohick, 1736-39.
Samuel Hull, Goose Creek, 1736-40.
John Bowie, Pohick, 1739-41.
John Richardson, Goose Creek, 1741-45.
John Barry, Pohick, 1743-75. Also at Alexandria, 1759-65; and at the Falls, 1761-65; and at Littlejohns, 1766.
Walter English, Upper, or Falls, 1743-45.
John Wybird Dainty, Upper, or Falls, 1745-53; and Alexandria, 1754-57.
John Allen, Goose Creek, 1745-46.

THE HISTORY OF TRURO PARISH

John Moxley, Goose Creek, 1747.
Thomas Evans, Goose Creek, 1748.
William Donaldson, Upper, or Falls, 1754-55.
John Lumley, Upper, or Falls, 1756-58; and Alexandria, 1758.
Thomas Lewis, Falls, 1759-60.
Elijah Williams, Littlejohns and Upper, or Payne's, 1766-69. Continued as Reader to 1771.
Benjamin H. West, Upper, or Payne's, 1769-72.
Daniel Atkins, Upper, or Payne's, 1772-77; and at Pohick, 1775-77.

Overseers of the Poor

The following is a list, in order, of the Overseers of the Poor, who succeeded the Vestries in caring for the poor of the County, and in certain other civil duties, from 1787 to 1802; from their records in the Vestry Book of Truro. Elections of Overseers were held every three years.

Peter Wagener	Presley Gunnell
Thomazen Ellzey	George Summers
John Fowler	Nicolas Fitzhugh
John Moss	Coleman Brown
Simon Sommers	Rezin Offutt
George Minor	Thomas Darne
Richard Simpson	Daniel Kitchen
John West	William Gunnell, Jr.
Roger West	John Dulin

THE HISTORY OF TRURO PARISH

Daniel Mc.Carty
Thomas Pollard
Thomas Gunnell
Thompson Mason
Charles Alexander
James Wiley

Francis Coffer
William Violett
Charles Thrift
William Middleton
Edward Dulin
James Douglass

Burgesses From Fairfax County

(Note: Each County was entitled to two Burgesses.)

Lawrence Washington, 1742-1749.
John Colvill, 1744-1748.
Richard Osborne, 1748-1749.
Hugh West, 1752-1754.
Gerrard Alexander, 1752-1755.
John West, 1756-1758, and 1761-1765, and 1766-1774.
George William Fairfax, 1756-1758.
George Johnston, 1758-1765.
George Mason, 1758-1761.
George Washington, 1765-1775.
Charles Broadwater, 1775.

Delegates to the Conventions 1775-1776.

March 1775. George Washington and Charles Broadwater.

July 1775. Charles Broadwater and George Mason.

December 1775. Charles Broadwater.

THE HISTORY OF TRURO PARISH

May 1776. John West, Jr., and George Mason. George William Fairfax was a Burgess for Frederick County, 1752-1755; Hugh West, 1756-1758; and George Washington, 1758-1765. Augustine Washington was a Burgess from Westmoreland. 1754-1758; William Fairfax a Burgess for Prince William before his promotion to the Council in 1744; and James Hamilton a Burgess for Loudoun for many years prior to 1771. All of those named above, with the exception of Lawrence Washington, Gerrard Alexander and George Johnston, were Vestrymen of Truro Parish.

This list is gathered from Stanard's "Virginia Colonial Register," except in the case of Col. John Colvill, whom Stanard supposes to have succeeded William Fairfax as Burgess for Prince William in 1744. But beside the testimony of the Rev. Charles Green that he was "a Burgess for this county" in 1744, the Journal of the House of Burgesses for that year indicates that he was a member of the House when the Writ for the election of a successor to Mr. Fairfax was issued. The matter is set at rest, however, by reference to "The Poll for Election of Burgesses for Fairfax County in the year 1744," on record in the Clerk's office. Capt. Lawrence Washington received 152 votes; Col. John Colvill, 151; Capt. Lewis Elzey, 101; and others a smaller number.

LIST OF VOTERS AT AN ELECTION OF BURGESSES IN FAIRFAX COUNTY IN 1744.

(Note:—Not all of these voters lived in Fairfax. An elector could vote in every country in which he owned a freehold of 25 acres of improved land, or 100 acres if unimproved. Each name appears twice on the poll lists, hence the variations in spelling.)

Benjamin Adams
Gabriel Adams
Gabriel Adams, Jun.
George Adams
Garrat Alexander
Bryant Aliston
John Allan
John Ashford
Michael Ashford
William Ashford
Francis Awbrey
John Aylatt
Robert Baker
John Ball
Moses Ball
William Barker
Wm. Barkley, or Buckley
William Bartlett
William Barton
Robt. Bates
H. Baugus, or Boggess
John Baxter
Thomas Beach
Col. Blackburn
Robert Boggess
W. Boylston, or Boilston
Thos. Bosman
William Bowling
Henry Brent
Chas. Broadwater
Guy Broadwater
John Bronaugh
Jeremiah Bronaugh
Thomas Brown
John Canady
Thos. Carney
Richard Carpenter

THE HISTORY OF TRURO PARISH

Job Carter
Wm. Champneys
Nathaniel Chapman
Josias Clapham
William Clifton
Catesby Cocke
John Cockerell
Richard Coleman
John Colvill
Samuel Comer
Jadwin Crutcher
Balden Dade
Townsend Dade
James Daniel
Sampson Darrell
Thomas Darus
William Davie
John Dickins
Robert Dickins
Joseph Dickson, or Dixon
Daniel Diskin, or Deskins
William Dodd
George Dunbarr
Blanchr. Duntan
Cornelius Eltenger
Thomas Ellett
John Elliott

Lewis Ellzey
Edward Emms
Col. Chas. Ewel(l)
Bertram Ewell
"Esquire" Fairfax
Jeremiah Fairhurst
Thomas Falkner
John Farguson
Thomas Ford
George Foster
Robert Forster
Daniel French Sen.
Daniel French (Jun.)
Joshua Garrett
Owen Gilmore
William Gladding
John Gladding
John Goram
Edward Graham
John Graham
John Grant
John Grantum
Charles Green
Charles Griffin
James Grimsley
Edward Grymes
William Grymes
John Guest
Henry Gunnell

THE HISTORY OF TRURO PARISH

William Gunnel	Joseph Jacobs
William Gunnel, Jun.	Abel Jenny, or Janney
William Hairsling	Amos Jenny, or Janney
William Hall, Sen.	Jacob Janney
William Hall, Jun.	James Jefferey
Thomas Hall	Ezekiel Jenkins
James Halley	James Jenkins
William Halling	John Jenkins
John Hamilton	William Jenkins
John Hampton	Thomas John
William Harle	James Keith
Samuel Harris, Sen.	Robert King
George Harrison	Richard Kirkland
Samuel Harrison	William Kirkland
Daniel Hart	William Kitchen
John Hartley	James Koon
John Hartshorne	John Koon
Francis Haugo, or Hago	Daniel Krouch
George Hester	James Lane
Robert Hester	Jacob Lawfull
John Hicherson	Abraham Lay
Jos. Higgerson	Thomas Lewis
Thomas Hicks	Thomas Lewis, Jun.
Thomas Hord	Stephen Lewis
John Hurst	Vincent Lewis
John Husk	Abraham Lindsey
Andrew Hutchinson	Moses Linton
Nimrod Hutt	Jacob Lucas
Powell Jackson	John Lucas

THE HISTORY OF TRURO PARISH

John Manley	Joseph Reid
Thomas Marshall	David Richardson
John Martin	James Roberts
Wm. Meckby, or Mc.Bee	John Roberts, Sen.
John Meade	John Roberts, Jun.
John Melton	William Roberts
John Minor	James Robinson
Thomas Monteith	John Robinson
William Moore	Richard Samford
Thomas Moseley	Robert Samford
Thomas Moxley	James Sanders, or
James Murray	Saunders
John Musgrove	Lewis Sanders
Christopher Neale	Edmond Sands
Anthony Neale	William Saunders
Henry Netherton	Thomas Scandall
Philip Noland	James Scott
Edward Norton	Benj. Sebastian
Richard Omohundro	John Shaddedin
Thomas Owsley	William Shortridge
William Peake	Isaac Simmonds
Thomas Penson	Baxter Simpson
William Perkins	George Simpson
Henry Peyton	Gilbert Simpson
Vall Peyton	Richard Simpson
George Platt	William Simpson
Nathaniel Popejoy	Jacob Smith
Christopher Pritchett	James Smith
Jacob Ramey	Thomas Smith
William Reardon	William Smith

James Spurr
Samuel Stone
John Straham
William Stribling
John Sturman
William Stutt
Francis Summers
Isaac Summers
John Summers
George Taylor
John Taylor
W. H. Terrett
David Thomas
Daniel Thomas
Robert Thomas
John Thompson
Samuel Tillett
Daniel Trammel
Garret, or Gerrard, Trammel
John Trammell
William Trammell
Francis Triplett
James Turley
John Turley

Fielding Turner
Michael Valandigam
Bond Veal
Zepheniah Wade
Samuel Warner
Lawrence Washington
Henry Watson
James Waugh
Hugh West
John West
Thomas West
Richard Wheeler
Thomas Whitford
Francis Wilks
Owen Williams
Walter Williams
William Williams, Sen.
William Williams, Jun.
Thomas Willis
William Winsor
Thomas Windsor
Thomas Wren
William Wright
James Wyatt
Daniel Young

Deed for Washington's Pew

The Deeds, nine in number, for the pews sold in Pohick Church, including that for the Minister's pew, are recorded in full in the records of the Clerk's Office of Fairfax County. Bishop Meade says they are probably the first of the kind ever executed in Virginia, as he had met with no hint of any such thing before in all his researches. The Deed for Washington's pews is as follows:

"THIS INDENTURE, made the twenty fourth day of February, in the year of our Lord one thousand, seven and seventy four, between the Vestry of Truro Parish, in the County of Fairfax, of the one part, and George Washington, of the same parish and county, Gent: of the other part: Whereas the said Vestry did, on the 5th. Day of June, in the year 1772, order sundry pews in the new Church on the upper side of Pohick to be sold, at the laying of the next Parish Levy, to the highest bidder for the benefit of the Parish; pursuant to which order the said pews were sold accordingly by the Vestry at the laying of the said Parish Levy on the 20th. day of November, in the same year; and the said George Washington, party to these presents, then purchased one certain pew in

THE HISTORY OF TRURO PARISH

the said Church for the price of sixteen pounds current money, to wit the pew numbered 28, situate between the two long Isles and adjoining the North Isle and the space before the Communion Table, and a certain Lund Washington, Gent; did at the same time purchase another certain pew in the said Church for the price of thirteen pounds ten shillings, current money, to wit, the pew numbered 29 situate between the two long Isles and adjoining the North Isle & the first mentioned pew, & whereas the said Lund Washington hath since relinquished and given up all his right and title to the said pew numbered 29 purchased by him as aforesaid unto the said George Washington, as by the proceedings and records of the said Vestry, Reference being thereunto had, may more fully and at large appear. Now this indenture Witnesseth that the said Vestry, for and in consideration of the sum of twenty nine pounds ten shillings current money, to them in hand paid, for the use of the said Parish, by the said George Washington, before the sealing and delivery of these presents, the receipt whereof is hereby confessed and acknowledged, have granted, bargained and sold, aliened and confirmed, and by these presents do grant, bargain and sell alien and confirm unto the said George Washington the said two pews in the said new Church lately built on the upper side of Pohick, in the said Parish of Truro and County aforesaid, numbered and sit-

THE HISTORY OF TRURO PARISH

uated as above mentioned, To have and to hold the said two pews above described unto the said George Washington, his heirs and assigns, to the only proper use and behoof of him, the said George Washington, his heirs and assigns forever. And the said Vestry, for themselves and their successors (Vestrymen of Truro Parish) do covenant and grant to and with the said George Washington, his heirs and assigns, that he the said George Washington, his heirs and assigns, shall and may forever hereafter peaceably and quietly have, hold and enjoy the said two pews above mentioned and described, without the Lawful Let, Hindrance, Interruption, or Molestation of any person or persons whatsoever. In witness whereof the Vestry now present (being a majority of the Members) have hereunto set their hands and affixed their seals the day and year first above written.

Signed, sealed and delivered in the presence of Wm. Triplett, Wm. Payne, Jr., John Barry, John Gunnell, Thomas Triplett.

> G. Mason (Seal)
> Daniel Mc.Carty (Seal)
> Alex. Henderson (Seal)
> T. Ellzey (Seal)
> Thos. Withers Coffer (Seal)
> Thos. Ford (Seal)
> Pet: Wagener (Seal)
> Martin Cockburn. (Seal)

"Received this twenty fourth day of February in the year 1774, of the within named George Washington the sum of twenty nine pounds, ten shillings, current money, being the consideration mentioned in the within Deed."

"Witness:" (The same signatures as above.)

Each Vestryman signed every Deed but his own, Washington's name always being second, except on the Deed to "George Mason of Gunston Hall," where it is first.

Pohick Church in the Olden Time

Washington as a Church-Goer

In a popular work entitled "The True George Washington," by the late Paul Leicester Ford, the brilliant author devotes a few pages only to a subject which demands a far more accurate and sympathetic treatment than is given to it, namely, Washington's religious training and habits. Referring to Washington's services as a Vestryman, it is acknowledged that he was "Quite active in Church affairs;" but in touching these the author not only repeats all the traditional errors which, for lack of authentic data, have been made by previous writers on this subject, but he falls into a number of new and strange ones, and becomes involved in a most curious labyrinth of inaccuracies. All these the foregoing pages will correct.

In discussing Washington's habits in regard to church attendance he first quotes the well known testimony of the Rev. Lee Massey, his pastor and close personal friend, as follows:—"I never knew so constant an attendant at Church as Washington. And his behavior in the house of God was ever so deeply reverential that it produced the happiest effect on my congregation, and greatly assisted me in my pulpit labors. No company ever

THE HISTORY OF TRURO PARISH

withheld him from Church. I have been at Mount Vernon on Sabbath morning when his breakfast table was filled with guests; but to him they furnished no pretext for neglecting his God and losing the satisfaction of setting a good example. For instead of staying at home, out of false complaisance to them, he used constantly to invite them to accompany him."

The author thereupon expresses the opinion that this was "Written more with an eye to its influence on others than to its strict accuracy;" and continues,—"During the time Washington attended at Pohick Church he was by no means a strict Church goer. His daily 'Where and How my Time is Spent' enables us to know exactly how often he attended Church, and in the year 1760 (?) he went just sixteen times and in 1768 he went fourteen, these years being fairly typical of the period 1760-1773."

As to the veracity of the Rev. Mr. Massey, whose testimony is so summarily set aside as disingenuous, we have the witness of his friends and neighbors, the Vestrymen of his Parish, who, as we have seen, certified over their own signatures to "His moral character and unexceptionable life and conversation." He seems indeed to have been a man of almost super-conscientiousness. He retired from the practice of law because, as his grandson, Col. J. T. Stoddert, a gentleman of the highest standing, who remembered him well,

THE HISTORY OF TRURO PARISH

states, "His conscience would not suffer him 'to make the worse appear the better reason,' and to uphold wrong against right. He tried to follow the lead of Chancellor Wythe, to examine cases placed in his care and to accept the good and reject the bad. It proved a failure, and he withdrew from practise. He recommended me to read law," he continues, "but earnestly opposed my pursuing it as a vocation. He was a good judge of character. He loved virtue and hated vice intensely. His integrity and honour were of the highest order, and he detested all meanness and double dealing with his whole heart."

Such was the character borne by Mr. Massey, who certainly had the best opportunity possible to know the facts in the case. And his statement agrees with that of others who, to go no further afield, were members of Washington's household. Mrs. Custis, who spent two years at Mount Vernon, testifies to "His extraordinary punctuality in attending Church and his reverent behavior there." And his ward, George Washington Parke Custis, of Arlington, wrote of him: "Washington was a strict and decorous observer of the Sabbath. He always attended divine service in the morning, and read a sermon or some portion of the Bible to Mrs. Washington in the afternoon." Mr. Custis is speaking of the period when Washington was President and had opportunity to attend Church regularly.

THE HISTORY OF TRURO PARISH

Figures standing alone are often seriously misleading, and those by which the testimony of Mr. Massey is sought to be impeached need some explanation. In the first place it is not quite certain that we can gather from Washington's diary "Exactly how often he attended Church." The customary and habitual is just what is usually omitted from a journal in which the record of a day is compressed within the compass of a few lines. A careful reading of this diary, kept for some years on the blank pages of interleaved almanacs and afterwards in small note-books, will show that while at home at Mount Vernon it was chiefly a record of the company he entertained, of his visits to his friends, of his surveys, his adventures in the hunting field, etc. On Sundays he would sometimes mention going to Church quite incidentally, and it is seen that for a month or two he attended about as regularly as services were held. Then for two or more months perhaps there will be no mention of Church at all, and no explanation of why he did not attend if he did not. But when, for instance, he "Dined at Belvior" with such and such guests he might very well have gone to Church on the way, or the neighbors he had to dinner he would quite likely have brought from Church with him. The more usual record for Sundays, however, is "At home all day," or "At home all day alone." This would seem conclusive until we find that it is also a common formula for week days on which

THE HISTORY OF TRURO PARISH

there was nothing of special note to record. It may simply mean that he dined at home without company; and especially so if he failed to make the entry on Sunday night but deferred it until he would be at his desk on Monday. Very occasionally he gives a reason why he was "prevented from Church."

But even if we grant that the above estimate of Washington's attendance at Church is substantially correct, other considerations must be borne in mind or our conclusions will be wholly at fault. It must be remembered that from 1760 to 1765 there was but one minister in the whole of Fairfax County, and he an old man in failing health. Mr. Green ministered alternately at three Churches, situated at a distance of about nine, ten, and eighteen miles respectively from Mount Vernon. This would allow him to preach seventeen or eighteen times in a year at Pohick. After the division of the Parish Mr. Massey had but two Churches and could preach twenty-six times a year at each, when the weather, the numerous water courses, and the state of the primitive roadways through marsh and forest permitted a congregation to gather from distances of from five to fifteen miles. Residents of Fairfax can appreciate what eighteen miles, going and coming, in the Mount Vernon "chariot" or even on horseback, must have meant; and can still understand the statement of Mrs. Nellie Custis Lewis that Washington attended Church "When the weather and roads permitted." Moreover Washington was absent from home for several months of each year, frequently in the wilds of western Virginia or on the Ohio. While visiting relatives in the lower counties he mentions frequently the Churches he attended, probably as interesting memoranda, and the same was the case when he was in Philadelphia. At the Berkeley Springs he twice "attended Church forenoon and afternoon." At Fredericksburg he "Went to prayers (lay reading) and dined afterwards at Col. Lewis." On hearing that the smallpox had broken out among his servants in Frederick, he starts at once to visit them and "Took Church on my way to Colemans." These and many such references indicate his habit. The argument from silence is never a very safe one, and his frequently omitting to mention going to Church in the regular routine of life at Mount Vernon does not, we think, prove that he was "By no means a strict Church goer," especially in view of the conditions existing.

It is interesting to note that twice within two weeks Washington makes record of having stood as Sponsor at the baptism of infants. According to the best evidence we have he was a regular Communicant during the period under discussion. In 1770 and in 1772 he mentions being at Church on Christmas day, which was always a Communion occasion.

THE DISESTABLISHMENT OF THE CHURCH IN VIRGINIA

To one of the old Vestrymen of Truro has been accorded by universal acclaim the title of Father of his Country, chiefly because of his pre-eminent leadership in her struggle for Independence. To another of these Vestrymen belongs the title of the Father of Religious Liberty. It is to George Mason that religion in America is indebted for the first clear and certain note proclaiming her right to be free, proceeding not from the bias of the partisan but from the wisdom of profound statesmanship. To him, too, more than to any other, the Church in Virginia owes her emancipation from the bonds of her vassalage to the State; bonds which had been her support once, and on which she still leaned with a woeful persistency, but which had almost crushed out her very life. From the dawn of American independence Mason saw not only the political necessity and the inherent justice of the complete separation of the Church from the State, but must have recognized also, with many others, that the existence of the Church of which he was a devoted adherent would ultimately depend upon her being freed from her political dependence and forced to rely upon the voluntary and intelligent support of her own children. Having adopted these views he pursued them to the end with a consistency and clearness of vision which was rare among his contemporaries.

The various Acts of the General Assembly by which the complete disestablishment of the Church was brought about were the following.

On the 12th of June, 1776, the State Convention, composed almost wholly of Churchmen, adopted without a dissenting voice, that famous "Declaration of Rights" which declared in its concluding article "That religion, or the duty which we owe to our CREATOR, and the manner of discharging it, can be directed only by reason and conviction, not by force or violence, and therefore all men are equally entitled to the free exercise of religion, according to the dictates of conscience; and that it is the mutual duty of all to practice Christian forbearance, love, and charity, towards each other." This "Bill of Rights," as it is usually called, was from the pen of Mason, and while it is quite possible that some in the Convention failed to perceive its full significance, it led, as it was mean to lead, to the withdrawal by the State of all support or supervision of religion.

The first General Assembly of the Commonwealth under the new Constitution met in October, 1776. Among its earliest Acts was the one

THE HISTORY OF TRURO PARISH

entitled, "An Act for exempting the different societies of Dissenters from contributing to the support and maintenance of the church as by law established, and its ministers, and for other purposes therein mentioned." Mason was Chairman of the Committee which brought in this Act, and it is supposed to have been written by his own hand. The Act is very long, almost every section having its own explanatory preamble. The first section repeals within this Commonwealth all Acts of Parliament directed against dissent or dissenters. The second exempts all dissenters from the established Church from all levies, taxes, and impositions whatever towards supporting and maintaining the said Church or its ministers. The Vestries, however, could still levy on all tithables for arrears in the salaries of ministers, for parochial engagements already entered into, and for the poor. Section four contains this important provision: "That there shall in all time coming be saved and reserved to the use of the Church as by law established the several tracts of Glebe lands already purchased, the churches and chapels already built,—all books, plate, and ornaments, belonging or appropriated to the use of the said church," and to each parish all private donations which may have been made to it. The next sections reserve for future determination, when the opinion of the country shall be better known, the question whether the support of ministers and teachers of the gospel of the different denominations shall be provided for by a general assessment or be left to voluntary contributions. And because the support of the clergy might fall too heavily on the members of the established Church in some parishes under the exemptions allowed dissenters, they were left to be supported for the present by voluntary contributions, and all acts for the support of the clergy by levies were suspended until the end of the next session of the Assembly. The remaining sections provide for taking lists of tithables.

The act for the support of the clergy continued to be suspended from time to time by the Assembly until the session of October, 1779, when so much of that act, and of every other act, as provided for salaries for the ministers of the Church of England, and authorizing levies for the same, was finally repealed.

The question between assessments and voluntary contributions was, however, still undecided. During the session of Assembly beginning October, 1784, a measure was introduced known as the Assessment Bill, providing for the legal support of ministers and teachers of religion of all denominations by a general assessment upon the people of the State. It was supported by Edmund Randolph, Patrick Henry, Richard Henry Lee, John Page, Edmund Pendleton and others, while a determined opposition was led by James Madison.

THE HISTORY OF TRURO PARISH

When the measure was about to pass Madison succeeded in having the final vote deferred until the next session. In the meantime, at the urgent suggestion of Mason, Nicholas and others, he prepared the famous "Memorial and Remonstrance" which was printed and circulated broadcast for signatures. Of these it received so many that at the following session of the Assembly the bill was readily defeated, and the principle of the support of religion by voluntary contributions was tacitly adopted.

Mason was active in circulating the Remonstrance, and among others he sent a copy to General Washington, his late fellow Vestryman. Washington wrote him in reply from Mount Vernon, Oct. 3rd, 1785: "Although no mans sentiments are more opposed to *any kind* of restraint upon religious principles than mine are, yet I must confess that I am not amongst the number of those who are so much alarmed at the thought of making people pay toward the support of that which they profess, if of the denomination of Christians, or declare themselves Jews, Mohammedons, or otherwise, and thereby obtain proper relief." But he thought the bill unfortunate at that time, and that it would be impolitic to make it a law.

The fight over this measure was one of the most strenuous and persistent that had ever engaged the Virginia Legislature. That it should have been advocated by so many great Statesmen and devoted Churchmen is a surprise to us at this day. The tradition and custom of many centuries was hard to be overcome, and the maintenance of religion without the sanction and support of the government in some form was to them an untried experiment, and of very doubtful success. Their opportunism was the child of their fears for religion and the Church.

But the public sentiment manifested in the response to the Remonstrance paved the way for the adoption of the Statute of Religious Freedom, inspired by Mason, written by Jefferson, and passed through the efforts of Madison. This bill had been reported in 1779 by the Committee appointed in 1776 for the revisal of the laws, consisting of Thomas Jefferson, George Wythe, George Mason, Edmund Pendleton, and Thomas Ludwell Lee, all of them old Vestrymen of the Church. Mr. Mason resigned from the Committee on the ground that he was no lawyer, and Mr. Lee died, before the report was made, but not until the plan of the work was settled and in a considerable degree carried into execution. This act, however, was not passed until 1785. The kernel of this famous bill, the "first act of religious freedom that ever passed a legislative assembly on the face of the earth," is contained in the words,— "That no man shall be compelled to frequent or support any religious worship, place, or ministry whatsoever,—but that all men shall be free to pro-

THE HISTORY OF TRURO PARISH

fess, and by argument to maintain, their opinion in matters of religion," &c.

The real disestablishment of the Church had occurred a year before in the "Act for Incorporating the Protestant Episcopal Church." This was passed in response to a petition of the Clergy, who, it would appear, desired to be themselves incorporated. But the Assembly would have none of this, and formed the minister and Vestry of each parish respectively a body corporate and politic, empowered to hold, acquire, and dispose of property for the use of the Church, and to make rules and orders for managing its temporal affairs. All present vestries were dissolved, and the method of electing the Vestries every three years is prescribed. All former acts relating to the powers or duties of vestries or ministers, and all acts touching upon doctrine, discipline, or forms of worship are repealed. The vestries were authorized to regulate all the religious affairs of the Church in Convention, to consist of two deputies from each parish, of whom the minister, if there was a minister, should be one. This Act was repealed two years later, but not until under its sanction the first Convention of the Church met, and the Diocese of Virginia was organized, May 18th, 1785.

So far the legislation affecting the Church had been guided, and in large part induced, by Her own sons, nourished at her side. Of that which followed another story might be told. The repeal,

THE HISTORY OF TRURO PARISH

in 1799, of all laws relating to "the late protestant episcopal church," (sic), the Act of 1802 confiscating the glebes, solemnly saved and reserved for the use of the said Church by two previous Acts of the Assembly, and claiming the right, though forbearing to exercise it, of confiscating the church buildings also, and the persistent refusal through many years to allow the Church to hold charitable funds or secure incorporation for her educational institutions; these show an animus which we rejoice to believe has almost disappeared, giving way to the sweeter claims of reason and charity.

LATER HISTORY OF POHICK CHURCH

Upon the organization of the Diocese of Virginia in the year 1785 no representative appears in the Convention from Truro Parish, nor does the name of the Parish appear on the Convention journals for more than half a century except once in a list of the parishes as divided into Presbyterial Districts. What occasional services, if any, were held in Pohick Church after the death of the Rev. Mr. O'Neill in 1813 we know not, until the silence is broken in 1838 by Bishop Meade in the report to the Convention from which extracts have already been given by Dr. Slaughter. To the same Convention the Rev. William P. C. Johnson reports, as Rector of Pohick Church, Truro Parish,—"It has been nearly two years since the minister of this Parish first commenced regular services in a Church, which, for a number of years, has resounded the echoes of the beasts of the field, instead of the prayers and praises of rational creatures. Owing to the dilapidated condition of the Parish Church his services have hitherto been only occasional. An effort is now being made to restore this Church to a comfortable condition, and the hope is entertained that ultimate good may

THE HISTORY OF TRURO PARISH

result from religious services in this hitherto moral waste of the Lord's vineyard." In 1841 he makes his last report, and adds "The minister of Truro Parish respectfully reports that the venerable Church edifice in which he officiates has been rescued from further decay and dilapidation." He makes no mention of the number of Communicants, but during the four years of his ministry there he baptized four white and eighteen colored infants, and officiated at eight marriages and four burials. He rendered occasional services at old Aquia Church in Stafford County and in the old Court House at Dumfries in Prince William. He was also employed as a tutor for the children of the last Mrs. George Mason, of Gunston Hall.

After Mr. Johnson's retirement the Church was sometimes opened for Divine service by Students from the Theological Seminary, with perhaps occasional visits from the Professors. The Methodists also preached there from time to time. In 1861 the Rev. R. T. Brown, of Fairfax C. H. reported that he had "Also taken charge of Pohick Church, near Mount Vernon, with fair prospects of success." But the outbreak of war made his ministry there a short one.

When the war was over it was found that Pohick had fared comparatively well, for there was left of it the walls, the roof and the ceiling. Of the interior woodwork there also remained the original cornice, while the stone font was afterwards dis-

THE HISTORY OF TRURO PARISH

covered in a neighboring farmyard where it had been used as a watering trough. Of its rehabilitation and consecration Bishop Johns wrote a few months before his death:—

"October 3d. 1875. I consecrated Pohick Church. Morning service by the Rev. Dr. Packard and the Rev. Dr. McIlhenny. Sermon by myself. This venerable building, in the location and erection of which General Washington was so active, was for many years the Parish Church of the family at Mount Vernon. It was during the late war shamefully damaged by its military invaders, who left it to crumble under the wasting influences of the weather, and to be carried off at pleasure by any one who fancied its material for private use. So, after the war of the Revolution, disappeared the church in which the "Father of his Country" was said to have been christened, and such seemed to be the doom of the church of his manhood, but its sad condition came to the knowledge of a generous Christian gentleman of New York, who enquired, then came and looked, and then never intermitted his efforts till the ruin was thoroughly repaired. A new chancel with all its appropriate furniture and a handsome communion service was provided, a font in front and a convenient robing room on one side of the chancel and a good pipe organ on the other. The restoration was complete, and the large congregation now assembled were gladdened by the presence

THE HISTORY OF TRURO PARISH

of the benefactor to whose sympathy and services they were so largely indebted, and who was now with them uniting in the consecration of the venerable building which he had been the honored agent in rescuing from ruin and preserving for their great benefit and the honour and worship of God. Until an ordained minister can be procured to officiate regularly for this congregation stated services will be rendered by students of the Seminary appointed for the purpose."

In September, 1881, the Rev. Samuel A. Wallis, newly ordained, took charge of Pohick, and from this moment the real revival of its life began. He found but ten Communicants. But his faithful work among the people of a widely scattered community soon resulted in gathering a large and interested congregation, to whom he ministered for thirteen years. A rectory was secured and other parish property added, and the active interest of the Mount Vernon Ladies' Association was enlisted in the church. Mr. Wallis resigned in 1894. Bishop Newton thus speaks of his ministry there: "The history of old Pohick Church for the past thirteen years, its resuscitation and progress, speaks with no uncertain sound in favor of a long and faithful pastorate. When Rev. S. A. Wallis entered upon the work as a Deacon it was one of the least promising fields in the Diocese. He left it, when elected a Professor in the Theological Seminary, with the church building in good con-

THE HISTORY OF TRURO PARISH

dition, a comfortable rectory, and the number of Communicants increased tenfold. The Sunday School of nearly one hundred scholars presented a most cheering outlook for the future."

Mr. Wallis continued his oversight of the congregation until the Rev. Henry F. Kloman took charge in the summer of 1895. He remained two years, and was succeeded in October, 1897, by the Rev. Everard Meade, the present beloved Rector. Under him the work, which has long been in contemplation, of a real restoration of the interior of the Church to its original appearance and beauty, has progressed and is in large part completed. The chancel, pulpit and the principal pews are now reproduced as exactly as possible as they were when the Church was received by the Vestry from the hands of Col. George Mason in 1774. The pews in the rear of the building alone remain to be restored. In this work the Rector and Vestry have been generously aided by the Mount Vernon Association, the Daughters of the American Revolution, and other patriotic and antiquarian societies, as well as by individuals who have been interested in preserving the sacred memories which cluster around this sturdy old temple of God. The reopening of the Church after its restoration took place on Advent Sunday, 1906; the sermon being preached by the Rev. Dr.. S. A. Wallis.

Since the year 1873 the following gentlemen, in order of their election, have served on the Vestry

THE HISTORY OF TRURO PARISH

of Pohick Church: R. G. Nevitt, T. F. Chapman, Charles Landstreet, Charles Potter, J. H. Claggett, J. M. Lewis, Dr. N. B. Nevitt, Seth Kurhling, W. R. Ward, A. C. Landstreet, James Haslip, George Erskine, John Theisz, John K. Nevitt, Harrison H. Dodge, John Landstreet, Joseph Specht, L. G. Reid, Wm. M. Nevitt, R. W. Gaillard, J. P. H. Mason, Corbin Thompson, L. A. Denty, George N. Milstead, B. F. Nevitt, Dr. W. P. Caton.

The present Vestry consists of Messrs.. Thomas F. Chapman, William M. Nevitt, John Landstreet, N. B. Nevitt, M. D., W. P. Caton, M. D., J. P. H. Mason, Harrison H. Dodge, George N. Milstead, B. F. Nevitt, Corbin Thompson, L. A. Denty, and Luther G. Reid.

OLIVET CHURCH; TRURO PARISH. A Chapel bearing this name was for many years a Mission station in charge of the students of the Theological Seminary of Virginia. This was destroyed during the war. A second Chapel was built on the same site, and was consecrated by Bishop Johns, June 2d, 1872. Twenty years later the present Church was built on a different and better site, and was consecrated by Bishop F. M. Whittle, April 4th, 1898. Olivet became connected with Pohick in 1881, when the Rev. Mr. Wallis took charge of them, and has since remained under the care of the Rector and Vestry

THE HISTORY OF TRURO PARISH

of Pohick Church. It is situated near Franconia Station.

POHICK CHAPEL. This is a small Chapel, situated about four and a half miles northwest of Pohick Church, to which it belongs. It was built in 1903 through the efforts of the Rev. Everard Meade, and was consecrated by Bishop R. A. Gibson on October 12th of that year.

Zion Church, Truro Parish

This Church, at the county seat of Fairfax County, was founded in the year 1843 by the Rev. Richard Templeton Brown. Mr. Brown was at that time Rector of the Falls Church. In his report from that Church to the Diocesan Council of 1843 he makes the following note:

"Fairfax court-house. On the 8th of February last we had the pleasure of organizing a new congregation at this very destitute place, and prompt measures were adopted for the immediate erection of a plain and substantial Church. The edifice has been commenced, and, if not entirely finished, will be used during the present year. Some of the most influential citizens of the place and neighborhood are interested in the work; the ladies also are zealously engaged; and we trust that, by the blessings of God, the Church at this place will exert a wide and purifying influence. Communicants 5. Families who will be regularly connected with the Church, about 12." The services were at first held in the Court House, but when for some reason its use was forbidden Mrs. Daniel Rumsey of "Mount Vinyard," a Baptist lady, declared that she "could not see the Ark of the Lord refused a

THE HISTORY OF TRURO PARISH

shelter," and offered her parlor in which the congregation met until the Church was completed. She was the mother of Mr. William T. Rumsey, who gave the lot for the Church and was one of its first Vestrymen. Mr. Brown removed from the field during the following year, and was succeeded in a few months by the Rev. William F. Lockwood, who at first combined the work with that of St. Stephen's Church, Fauquier, but afterwards resigned the latter and took charge of the Falls Church. The Church was completed, and was consecrated by the Right Rev. William Meade, D. D., on the 28th of June, 1845, under the name of Zion Church. It was a frame building, of the same size as the present Church, and was the first Church of any kind erected in the village. At this time there were 14 Communicants. Mr. Lockwood remained as Rector until 1852 or 1853, when he removed to Maryland. Under his ministry St. John's Church, Centerville, was built, and was consecrated by Bishop John Johns, D. D., July 14th, 1851.

Occasional services were held by the Professors of the Theological Seminary until the Rev. R. T. Brown returned to his old charge in 1855, and remained Rector of Zion Church, in connection with the Falls and St. John's, until he and the greater part of his congregation were forced to flee from their homes in 1861, when Fairfax became involved in the maelstrom of war. Four years later,

THE HISTORY OF TRURO PARISH

when the people returned to their desolated homes, they found only the foundation of their Church remaining. It had shared the fate of perhaps a majority of the country churches in that beautiful section, where they "Made a solitude and called it peace." Early in the conflict it had been used as a storehouse for the munitions of war, and rapidly becoming dilapidated it had been finally torn down by Union soldiers to provide material for their winter quarters on a neighboring hillside.

There was no minister until February, 1867, when the Rev. W. A. Alrich was ordained to the diaconate and sent to undertake the work of resuscitating the Church at this point, in connection with Centerville, and Haymarket in Prince William County. He found 18 Communicants. Services were held in the Court House. He reported, however, "A deep interest manifested in religious matters, and a willingness to make every sacrifice for the sake of the Master and his cause. The people, in their impoverished condition, are now making an earnest effort to rebuild their Churches." On December 13th, 1868, Bishop Whittle visited the congregation and confirmed fourteen persons in the Court House. He reported the new Church as being under roof, but its completion delayed for want of funds, and adds, "I think there is no congregation in the Diocese more deserving of help than this, where the people have shown such a determination to help them-

THE HISTORY OF TRURO PARISH

selves." Mr. Alrich resigned, and was succeeded in June, 1869, by the Rev. William M. Dame, who remained during the year of his diaconate. The Rev. D. Hanson Boyden succeeded him in the summer of 1870, and gave the whole of his short ministry of fifteen months to this Parish. He resigned on account of failing health on October 1st, 1871, and died less than three months later. Bishop Johns said of him: "His ministry was short and emphatic. The distress which his early death caused to the people whom he served affords affecting evidence of his personal worth and ministerial fidelity and usefulness."

The Rev. John McGill took charge during the summer of 1872. The second Zion Church was now completed, and being furnished and freed from debt was consecrated by Bishop Johns on the 6th of December, 1875. It is a frame building and was erected on the foundation of the original Church at a cost of about $2,000. On the day following its consecration Christ Church at Chantilly was also consecrated. This, with the Church at Centerville, which was also rebuilt, though really in old Cameron Parish, were supposed to be in Truro and were under the charge of Mr. McGill. In 1884 these Churches, with that at Herndon and the mission at Clifton, were formed into a Parish called Upper Truro.

Mr. McGill resigned April 23d, 1878, and was succeeded by the Rev. Frank Page during the fol-

THE HISTORY OF TRURO PARISH

lowing summer. In the year 1882 the present Rectory property adjoining the Church was purchased for $2,600. Mr. Page resigned November 19th, 1889. During the earlier part of his rectorship he ministered at no less than five Churches, but after the formation of Upper Truro Parish his labors were confined to Zion and the Falls Churches. After his removal the Church remained vacant until July, 1890, when Mr. J. Cleveland Hall, formerly a Presbyterian minister, but now a candidate for orders in the Episcopal Church, came as a Lay-Reader and continued to officiate as such until his ordination to the Diaconate in June, 1891; after which he continued as minister-in-charge until July, 1892. During the following year services were held by Mr. W. A. R. Goodwin, candidate for orders, and other students from the Theological Seminary. In the summer of 1893 the Rev. Thomas D. Lewis became the minister, in connection with Trinity Church, Manassas; the old partnership with the Falls Church having been dissolved. Mr. Lewis remained until May, 1896, when failing health compelled him to resign. He was followed by the Rev. W. H. K. Pendleton, who served the same Churches until early in 1900, when, the work having outgrown the capacity of a single minister, he resigned Zion Church and confined his labors to the neighboring Parish. An alliance was then formed with the Church of the Holy Comforter at

THE HISTORY OF TRURO PARISH

Vienna, Fairfax County, now McGill Parish, and after some months the Rev. Albert R. Walker became the Rector. He continued until September, 1902, and was succeeded in June, 1903, by the Rev. Henry B. Lee, Jr., who remained nine months. On June 1st, 1904, the Rev. Edward L. Goodwin became Rector.

The destruction of all the Parish Records during the war of 1861 makes it impossible to give a list of the Vestrymen who served prior to that time. Among the families who formed the congregation of Zion Church in *ante-bellum* days were the Bakers, Balls, Chichesters, Fairfaxes, Fitzhughs, Furgussons, Gunnells, Hunters, Mosses, Ratcliffes, Ronks, Ryers, Stuarts, Terretts, Towners, Burkes, Coopers, Loves, Thomases, &c. The gentlemen of some of these families doubtless formed the Vestry of those days. Since 1872 the succession of Vestrymen has been as follows: William T. Rumsey, Thomas Moore, H. C. Fairfax, Albert Fairfax, M. D., O. W. Huntt, W. D. McWhorter, M. D., Joseph Cooper, James M. Love, Daniel McCarty Chichester, Gen. W. H. F. Lee, E. D. Ficklin, G. Pat Berkley, J. N. Ballard, John Peabody, Upton H. Herbert, Washington Terrett, W. P. Moncure, M. D., Robert E. Lee, Jr., S. Thornton Terrett, R. Ewell Thornton, Alex. C. Bleight, C. Vernon Ford, J. Conway Chichester, J. B. Bowman, R. Walton Moore, Thomas R. Keith, James P. Machen, Jr., Harry L. Burrows. Of these Mr.

THE HISTORY OF TRURO PARISH

O. W. Huntt, Mr. Joseph Cooper and Mr. James M. Love have served continuously on the Vestry for thirty-five years, equalling the record of those veteran Colonial Vestrymen, George Mason and Daniel Mc.Carty. Besides these the Vestry at present consists of Messrs. Moncure M. D., R. E. Lee, Thornton, Bleight, R. W. Moore, Keith, and Burrows.

CHAPEL OF THE GOOD SHEPHERD, TRURO PARISH. This Chapel, situated one and a half miles north of Burke's Station, grew out of Sunday School founded at Ashford school house many years ago by the Misses Fitzhugh and others, and continued chiefly by Mrs. Upton H. Herbert, under the Rectorship of the Rev. Frank Page. By the earnest efforts of Mrs. Herbert, began in 1882 and continued through more than a decade of years, the means were collected and the Chapel built. It was consecrated by Bishop John B. Newton, December 1st, 1896. The Rev. S. A. Wallis, of Pohick Church, held services for a number of years in the school house and afterward in the new building. Since 1894 it has been under the charge of the Rector and Vestry of Zion Church.

INDEX

NOTE: For many Proper Names not found in the Index see under Lists of Vestrymen, Processioners, Voters, etc., and throughout the book.

Acts of General Assembly, 2, 17, 22, 26, 28, 38, 40.
Adams, Gabriel, 4.
Alexandria, 30. First Church in, 30. Christ Church, 47, 97.
Alrich, Rev. W. A., 160.
Andrews, Rev. John, 48.
Ashford, Michael, 5.
Assessment Bill, 146.
Attorneys for Parish, 32, 49, 64.
Aubrey, Francis, 4.
Barnes, Abraham, 27.
Barry, Edward, 4. John, 49.
Baxter, James, 7.
Bill of Rights, 144.
Blackburn, Richard, 6. Family, 103.
Blumfield, Rev. Joseph, 15.
Boggess, Robert, 21.
Books, Ornaments, &c. for Churches, 15, 62, 67, 88.
Boyden, Rev. D. H., 161.
Braddock's Road, 23.
Broadwater, Charles, 4, 27ff.
Bronaugh, Jeremiah, 4ff.
Brown, Rev. R. T., 158.
Burgesses from Fairfax, List of, 126.
Cameron Parish, 22, 26, 161. Churches in, 22, 24.
Champneys, William, 25.
Chapel Above Goose Creek, 5.
Church, The Colonial, in Virginia, Introduction. Decay of, 96. Disestablishment of, 143.
Church Plate, 15, 61, 69, 145.
Church Wardens, Duties of, 16, 78. List of, 120. Become Overseers of the Poor, 93.
Clerks and Lay Readers, List of, 123.
Clerks of the Vestry, List of, 123.
Cockburn, Martin, 78, 116.
Coffer, Francis, 92. Thos. Withers, 44ff. Family, 118.
Cocke, Catesby, 9, 16.
Colchester, 31.
Colville, Col. John, 7ff., 127.
Contracts for Church Buildings, 51, 73.
Dame, Rev. W. M., 161.
De Butts, Rev. Lawrence, 5.
Delegates to State Convention, 1775-6, 126.
Deneale, William, 94.
Diocese of Virginia Organized, 149.
Dranesville, Church near, 24.
Ellzey, Lewis, 21, 127. Thomazen, 44ff.
Emms, Edward, 4ff.
Fairfax County formed, 17. Boundaries changed, 26.

INDEX

Fairfax Court House, 17, 158.
Fairfax Parish, 36. Contest over lines, 39. Final Act establishing, 40. Vestries elected, 44-5.
Fairfax, George William, 33ff, 127.
Lord Thomas, 1, 10.
William, 32-3, 127.
Falls Church, The first, or William Gunnell's, 5. The second, or "Upper" Church, 6ff. The third, or present Church, 34ff.
Farguson, John, 7.
Front in Pohick Church, 84, 152.
Forbes, Murray, 108.
Ford, Edward, 92. John, 44, Thomas, 44ff.
Ford, Paul Leicester, quoted, 6. 137.
French, Daniel, 21, 70ff.
Gardner, William, 44ff.
Gibson, John, 95.
Glebe, 8, 12, 28, 29, 31, 61.
Glebes, Confiscation of, 150.
Godfrey, William, 4.
Gold Leaf given by Washington and Fairfax, 81, 90.
Good Shepherd, Chapel of the, 164.
Goodwin, Rev. E. L., 163.
Grayson, William, 64. 113.
Green, Rev. Charles, 10. First Rector, 13ff., 141.
Gunnell's, William, Church, 5.
Hall, Rev. C., 162.
Hamilton, James, 27. 127.
Hamilton Parish, 2.
Henderson, Alexander, 44ff., 108. Family, 109.

Herbert, Mrs. U. H., 164.
Hereford, John, 4ff.
Holmes, Rev. John, 11.
Holy Communion, Elements for, 34, 66.
Hutchinson, Andrew, 21ff.
Induction, Right of, 57.
Johnson, Joseph, 7.
Johnson, Rev. W. P. C., 106.
Johnston, George, 38, 49, 115.
Keith, Rev. James, 12.
Kloman, Rev. H. F., 155.
Lee, Rev. H. B., Jr., 163.
Lee, Gen. R. E., his pew in Christ Church, Alexandria, 96.
Letters of Recommendation and Presentation, 10, 13, 55, 56, 59.
Lewis, John, 4. Lawrence, 111. Mrs. Nellie Custis, 100. 112. Thomas, 7. Rev. Thomas D., 162.
Linton, William, 44ff.
Littlejohn, Samuel, 47.
Lackwood, Rev. William F., 159.
London, Bishop of, 8, 10, 54.
Loudoun County formed, 26.
Mandamus served on Vestry, 25.
Mason, George, Vestryman and Church Warden, 27ff. Opposes change of site of Pohick, 64. Completes Church building, 84-85. His pews in, 87. Long service on the Vestry, 95-96. Father of religious liberty, 143.
Massey, Rev. Lee. Letters in favor of, 55. Second

INDEX

Rector, 59ff. Retirement, 93. Testimony of, as to Washington's attendance at Church, 137. Character, 138.
McCarty, Daniel, 27ff. Long service as Vestryman, 95. Daniel, Jr., 94. Dennis, 4.
McGill, Rev. John, 161.
McGill Parish, 3, 163.
Meade, Rev. Everard, 155.
Meade, Bishop William, quoted, 21, 63, 100, 104.
Minister, effort to obtain from England, 9.
Minor, John, 21.
Moore, Cleon, 94, 116.
Mount Vernon, 41, 112.
Northern Neck of Virginia, 1.
Occoquan Church, 5.
Olivet Church, 156.
O'Neill, Rev. Charles, 102.
Orphans bound to trades, 16.
Osborne, Richard, 4ff.
Overseers of the Poor, 93. List of, 124.
Overwharton Parish, 5.
Page, Rev. Frank, 161.
Parish Levies, 9, 15, 49, 65. Vestrymen not to collect, 77. For support of the church abolished, 93, 146.
Parishes formed from Truro, 3.
Payne, Edward, 44ff. William, 27.
Paynes Church, 50. Contract for building, 51. Later history and destruction of, 68.
Peake, William, 7ff.
Pendleton, Rev. W. H. K., 162.
Pews, assigned according to rank, 14, 27, 87. Sale of, in Pohick Church, 80ff. In Christ Church Alexandria, 97.
Physicians for the Poor, 25, 26, 66, 93.
Pohick Church, the Old, 5, 63. Repairs on, 16, 27.
Pohick Church, the present, 63. Discussion as to site for, 63. Plans for, 70. Contract for, 73. Lot for, 71, 77. Details in construction of, 79-90. George Mason completes it, 84-5. Pews sold, 83-5, 133. Other pews assigned, 87. Font in, 84. Books and ornaments for, to be imported by Washington, 88. Washington's attendance at, 99. Services after the Revolution, 100. Its decay, 104. Efforts at resuscitation, 106, 151. Consecration of, 153. Restoration now in progress, 155. Vestrymen, 156.
Pohick Chapel, 157.
Pollard, Thomas, 91.
Poor, Provision for the, 11, 16, 25, 32, &c.
Posey, John, 44ff.
Processioning of Lands, 18.
Processioners and Precincts, Lists of, 18, 28, 32, 62.
Reagan's, Michael, Church near, 6.
Religious Freedom, Mason's advocacy of, 143. Statute of, 148.
Rocky Run Chapel, 22.

INDEX

Ross, Hector, 60.
Rumsey, Wm. T., 159.
Salaries, of Ministers, 15, 93, 97, 145. Of Clerks and Readers, 9, 10, &c.
Scott, Rev. James, 45.
Sears, Wm. B., 88.
Slaughter, Rev. Dr. Philip, Introduction.
Sparks, Jared, referred to, 46, 64.
Sturman, John, 4ff.
Terrett, Wm. H., 22.
Tillett, Giles, 4.
Tithables, 10, 26, 91.
Tobacco as currency, 5, &c.
Tobacco House used as a Chapel, 48.
Trammel, John, 9.
Triplett, William, 92. Family, 119.
Truro Parish, Genesis of, 1. Old Vestry-Book of, 3. Boundaries of, 2, 26, 40. Churches in, 5, 6, 23, 50, 63. Division of, first, 26; second, 36-42. Decay of on suspension of levies, 93ff. Later history of, 151. Vestrymen of, Introduction, 44-45, 120, 156, 163.
Turley, John, 27.
Upper Truro Parish, 26, 161.
Vestry House, 27, 60, 69.
Vestry of Truro, The first, 4. Dissolved by the General Assembly, 20. The second, 21. Third, 44. Fourth, 45. Last Meeting, 96. Of present Churches, 156, 163.
Vestrymen, distinguished, Introduction. Training of, Ditto. Lists of, 4, 21, 44, 45, 120, 156, 163. Oaths and subscriptions of, 21. Long service of, 95, 164.
Vestries in Virginia, Introduction. Not of Churches but of parishes, 47. Dissolved, 149.
Voters, List of, in 1744, 128.
Wagener, Dr. Peter, 78. Peter, Jr., 91. Family, 110.
Waite, Thomas, 29ff.
Wallis, Rev. S. A., Introduction. 154.
Washington, George, Vestryman and Church Warden, 34, 35ff. Baptism, 6. Part taken by, toward building Falls Church, 34-6. In division of Parish, 41. Vestryman in only one Parish, 42. His lists of Vestrymen chosen, 1765, 44-45. On two Building Committees for Churches, 51, 72. Extracts from diary of, 67, 72, 99, 142. Did he draw plans for Pohick? 70. Choice of site for church, 64. Gives gold leaf for gilding, 81, 90. Purchase of pews in Pohick, 82, 87. Gives bond for price of, 89. Deed for, 133. Requested to import books and hangings for Pohick, 88. His Last Vestry, 89. Regularity of attendance at Vestry, 89. Resignation as Vestryman, 95. Buys pew in Christ Church, Alexandria, and

INDEX

was a parishioner there, 96-97. His memorandum of sale of pews, 97. Bond for pew rent, 97. Still attended Pohick when services there, 99. Regularity of his attendance at church, 99, 137. Distance from Churches, 141. Stands as Sponsor, 142. Views of, on Assessments for support of Religion, 147.

Washington, Augustine, 9, 10. Bushrod, 103. Edward, 15, 110. Lawrence, 9, 22. Lund, 95, 110.
Waugh, John, 95.
Weems, Rev. Mason L., 100.
West,, Hugh, 21ff. John, 21ff. John, Jr., 33. Mrs. Sybil, 34.
Wren, James, 70. Thomas, 27.
Zion Church, Fairfax, 158.

www.ingramcontent.com/pod-product-compliance
Lightning Source LLC
Chambersburg PA
CBHW070300230426
43664CB00014B/2595